SUNNY Stitches

Sweet & Simple Embroidery Projects
for Absolute Beginners

DEDICATION

This book is dedicated to my grandma, Marilyn Rockafellow, who inspired me and many others to live a creative, faithful, and joyful life. And to my children, Adam and Esme, who are the greatest two sunshines I'll ever know. I love you both so much!

Text, pattern illustrations, and photography (except where noted below) copyright © 2022 by Celeste Johnston. All other photography and diagrams © 2022 by Better Day Books, Inc.

Publisher: Peg Couch
Editor: Katie Weeber
Cover/Book Designer: Michael Douglas

Diagrams on pages 144, 145, 146, 147, 148 by Mollie Johanson
Photography on pages, 4, 5, 13, 15, 17, 39, 45, 51, 57, 65, 71, 77, 85, 93, 99, 106, 111, 119, 125, 131, 137 by Jason Masters / Photostyling by Lori Wenger

ISBN: 978-0-7643-6414-3
Printed in China
Library of Congress Control Number: 2022932581
Copublished by Better Day Books, Inc. and Schiffer Publishing, Ltd.

Schiffer Publishing
4880 Lower Valley Road
Atglen, PA 19310
Phone: 610-593-1777
Fax: 610-593-2002
Email: Info@schifferbooks.com
Web: www.schifferbooks.com

This title is available for promotional or commercial use, including special editions. Contact info@schifferbooks.com for more information.

SUNNY Stitches

Sweet & Simple Embroidery Projects for Absolute Beginners

CELESTE JOHNSTON
Lemon Made Shop

BETTER DAY BOOKS®
HAPPY • CREATIVE • CURATED

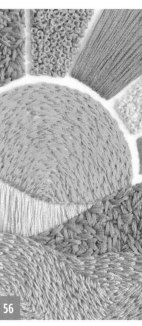

Contents

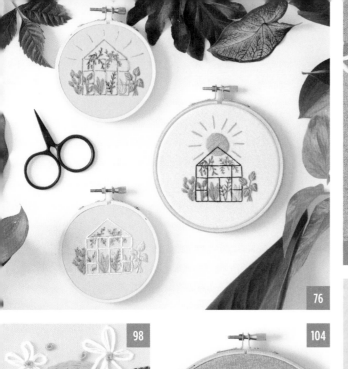

76

Fresh as a Daisy

84

Meet me at the Farmers' Market

92

98

104

110

118

124

130

MY HAPPY PLACE

136

Welcome

Hi there!

I'm so glad you picked up this book! It means the world to me that you would join me in the fulfilling, creative, and therapeutic hobby of embroidery. If you're brand new to embroidery, you have so much joy coming your way! I think you'll figure out pretty quickly that embroidery is an absolutely charming and captivating hobby.

If embroidery is already a beloved craft for you, I'm so glad you're here too. I hope you gain a new insight or two, and I'm so appreciative that you want to make something new today with my patterns!

I have been a crafter all my life, but it wasn't until more recently that I discovered a love for embroidery. I was drawn in at the first stitch when I realized how much it encouraged me to slow down and create something beautiful with my hands. I've learned the craft has other perks too.

The gentle weaving of the needle through the fabric is a restorative, therapeutic process that will keep your hands engaged for hours, leaving you with a feeling of accomplishment. Selecting your subject matter, fabric, and floss colors gives you endless creative freedom. And this craft is very practical.

Embroidery supplies are inexpensive, minimal, and portable. For someone who may have only a few moments a day to devote to a hobby, you'll soon understand that the setup is convenient, and your projects can be tucked away or taken on the go fairly easily. Stitching outside at a park or at a coffee shop with a friend is one of my favorite ways to enjoy this hobby.

My inspiration for the lighthearted designs in this book comes from how I would wish to spend a Saturday—a walk through the farmers' market, enjoying a delicious brunch, a peaceful and tranquil hike, or picking a few wildflowers along a country road.

As you work through the projects, please keep in mind that embroidery is an opportunity to express your creativity and is meant to be a joyful part of your day. You can follow the patterns and colors just as I created them or play with any colors and alterations that you are drawn to. Your embroidery may not look exactly like mine, and that's okay. Mistakes and do-overs are part of the process, and because embroidery is such a forgiving craft, don't be hard on yourself. Take your time, take care of yourself, and enjoy the process!

Love,

Celeste

Meet the Author

What do you love about embroidery?

I love the warmth and texture a piece of embroidery brings to a space. I also love how easy it is to sit down and pick up without mess or preparation. However, it's the process that draws me in. The rhythmic motion of filling in patterns with beautiful colors is very therapeutic. It's a hobby that has been engaging women for hundreds of years, and I love being a part of that heritage.

Where do you live?

My family and I live right outside Austin, Texas, and I am originally from Peoria, Illinois.

Where do you stitch? Do you have a designated studio?

I share a home workspace with my husband, Taylor. I use my desk for sketching, transferring patterns, choosing floss colors, and working on the business side of my art. But I usually stitch on my comfy couch in front of the TV, outside watching my kids play, or in a coffee shop listening to podcasts, audiobooks, or phenomenal playlists that my husband creates for me.

Check out Celeste's other book, *Freshly Stitched: Modern Embroidery for Absolute Beginners!*

You have a significant following on Instagram; can you tell us how that platform inspires your work?

I love being a part of the global embroidery community through Instagram. It's incredible to see the variety of art created with the simple medium of needle and thread. My Instagram account started as a way to share with friends, and it grew organically to a community of more than 70,000. I'm pretty introverted and never expected to have such an audience, and now—two books! I think it is enjoyed by so many because I share tutorials and tips for embroidery. I try to be consistent in my style and authentic to myself, sharing highs and lows. I engage with my "Instagram friends" as if they are friends in real life, having conversations about stitching, life, plants, and everything in between.

In addition to being a busy designer, artist, and entrepreneur, you are a mama to two adorable kiddos. How do you balance it all?

Being a mom, artist, author, and entrepreneur is a lot to balance. I have to carefully choose what I commit to, which means getting comfortable saying no when something doesn't fit or bring me joy. I sometimes struggle with meeting the demands of my family and work. Ultimately, I put my family's needs first because I recognize that these years are fleeting. Thankfully, I have a supportive husband who has an equal hand in parenting our kids.

What do you hope readers will get from this book?

I hope they will feel empowered to create something new with the patterns and instructions I have provided. I hope they make a life long connection with embroidery. And, I hope they gain as much happiness from this fulfilling craft as I have.

Celeste's Stitching Playlist

"Love Grows (Where My Rosemary Goes)"
BY EDISON LIGHTHOUSE

"Boca Chica"
BY MUNYA

"Texas Sun"
BY KHRUANGBIN & LEON BRIDGES

"Be My Baby"
BY THE RONETTES

"Emmylou"
BY FIRST AID KIT

"Losing You"
BY SOLANGE

"Big Sur"
BY THE BEACH BOYS

"Summer Girl"
BY HAIM

"Oh Yoko!"
BY JOHN LENNON

"Tender as a Tomb"
BY TENNIS

"Our House"
BY CROSBY, STILLS, NASH & YOUNG

"Bike Dream"
BY ROSTAM

"Long Lost"
BY LORD HURON

"(What a) Wonderful World"
BY SAM COOKE

"Our Deal"
BY BEST COAST

"La Vie en Rose"
BY LUCY DACUS

"Solstice"
BY THE ANTLERS

"With Arms Outstretched"
BY RILO KILEY

Getting Started

If this is your first experience with embroidery, the tutorials in this section will provide all the information you need to get started. Be sure to stitch the sample project to try out all the stitches and develop your skills. For even more information, check out the appendix on page 142.

Let's start stitching!

Fabric

When you set out to embroider a design, the first element to consider is your background fabric. This is the foundation of your project that will allow your beautiful stitching to shine. Choosing the wrong fabric will result in puckering or stretching, which would be such a disappointment after putting your time and effort into stitching the design. My best advice is to keep it simple—choose a common quilting cotton or linen fabric with no elasticity. To expand on that, here are a few details to keep in mind.

Type

If you're a beginner, I recommend a loose-weave fabric such as muslin or osnaburg. These fabrics will help you practice the basics of stitching because the needle and floss can slide through them so easily. They're inexpensive, come in natural or white colors, and are readily available at any craft or fabric store.

My favorite fabric for beginners and experienced stitchers alike is Kona cotton. If that's not available to you, choose any high-quality quilting cotton, which will have a high thread count, feel very smooth, and suit nearly any embroidery project. I also frequently stitch on linen or linen blend fabrics.

Embroidery on thick or stiff fabrics such as denim or canvas is possible, but these are a bit of a challenge to stitch through. Avoid any fabrics with stretch because they will warp your designs.

Color

Choosing just the right colors for your projects can be such a fun exercise in creativity. When it comes to fabric, I prefer stitching on solid colors, but feel free to get adventurous and choose a fabric with a subtle pattern.

When I stitch on a light color, such as white or peach, I like to double up the fabric to create an opaque background. It's slightly easier to transfer patterns onto light fabrics than dark ones, which is something to keep in mind when choosing your fabric colors.

While transferring the pattern may be more challenging, it's possible to stitch on dark fabrics. For these fabrics, white carbon transfer paper or fabric stabilizer will be your friend!

Preparing Your Fabric

Before you start stitching, there are just a few things you'll need to do to prepare your fabric.

- If your fabric has substantial wrinkles, iron it before transferring your pattern onto it.
- If you're stitching on fabric that will be removed from the hoop once the project is complete (a shirt, for example) preshrink it by washing it before stitching.
- Decide if you want to use one or two layers of the fabric, depending on its thickness and color.
- Use a good pair of fabric scissors to trim your fabric to size. I recommend trimming your fabric into a square with 2 to 3 inches of excess on all sides.

Floss

You know you love embroidery when you behave like a kid in a candy store in the thread aisle, adding to your basket each and every color that catches your eye. It's a good thing that embroidery floss (or thread) is inexpensive, because you'll want to have a variety of colors on hand to experiment with different combinations.

Type

Basic cotton embroidery floss is sold in skeins of six strands loosely banded together. For each of the projects in this book, you'll need one skein or less of each color noted in the supplies list. The project instructions also note how many strands of each color you'll use to stitch the different areas of a design. Read about how and why to split your floss in the tutorial on page 24.

In addition to the ever-popular and versatile cotton floss, you'll find specialty flosses such as pearl (perle), satin, metallic, tapestry wool, or silk. These are fun to incorporate into your pieces, and we'll experiment with them in the Fresh as a Daisy project on page 84 and the Brilliant Butterfly project on page 130.

There are quite a few different brands of embroidery floss widely available, but for this book, I used DMC floss. The specific color numbers are listed in the Floss Color Index on page 150. Feel free to use any floss brand and colors you prefer.

Storage

There are several ways to store embroidery floss. Some stitchers like to wind their floss on small white bobbins and store them in a thread organizer. Others use clothespins or wooden spools to keep their floss neat and tangle-free.

TIP: Keep long floss scraps to use for other projects. I keep a little jar at my workspace for these useful leftovers.

Embroidery Tools

One of the many reasons embroidery is a beloved and timeless hobby is because the necessary tools are inexpensive and easily accessible. If you're a crafty person, you probably have most of these essentials in your home already. Here are the tools you'll want on hand in your embroidery basket.

Hoops. Embroidery hoops are made of a metal tightening mechanism and two rings that grasp your fabric and hold it taut, creating the right surface for stitching. You can find embroidery hoops in all sizes, but for this book, you'll only need 4", 5", and 6" hoops. You can purchase hoops at your local craft store. Also keep an eye out for them while shopping at thrift stores.

Scissors. Keep two types of scissors on hand in your embroidery basket: fabric shears and embroidery scissors. The shears are for cutting your fabric to size. The small and very sharp embroidery scissors are for trimming threads, especially in compact spaces.

Needles. For the projects in this book, basic size 5 embroidery needles are perfect, but you may want to try a few different sizes. Purchase a pack of assorted-size embroidery needles so you can experiment. I like to use smaller needles when I'm working with one or two strands of floss only. I have learned tapestry or crewel needles are necessary when working with yarn or tapestry wool. If you're adding beads to a piece of embroidery, you'll want to find a beading needle or a needle with a shaft and eye narrow enough to fit through the beads.

Needle minder or pin cushion. You'll want to have a place to set aside your needle when you need to take a break or change floss colors. Use a magnetic needle minder or a pin cushion to keep your needle from getting lost.

Needle threader. This optional tool can be very helpful for threading your needle.

Glue. Fabric-safe glue can be used to finish the back of your embroidery project.

Cardstock. Thick paper like cardstock is useful for finishing the back of an embroidery project.

Transfer pens. There are several types of fabric transfer pens available to you. I like to use a black heat-erasable pen for most projects. Once you finish stitching, you use a hair dryer to erase any visible pen marks. You may also like a blue water-soluble marker, which washes away with water once you're finished stitching. A chalk pencil is handy for transferring patterns onto dark fabrics.

Carbon paper. Tracing patterns onto dark or thick fabrics is difficult. Instead, I use these tissue-thin transfer sheets. You'll find them in the needle arts aisle of your local craft store.

Mixed Media

Throughout this book, I'll guide you through embroidery techniques and stitching to create many beautiful finished pieces. But embroidery is not solely limited to fabric and thread. This book will also walk you through several simple techniques to add color and dimension to your work, using paint, colored pencils, fabric appliqué, and beads.

Experiment and have fun exploring different types of media mixed with embroidery. Don't be overwhelmed by these embellishments and additions—omit them or use them only as you wish as you advance in your stitching skills. Whenever a new medium is introduced in a project, I'll offer a floss alternative that you can use in its place. Once you have a little introduction to working with these different media, you'll see that the possibilities are endless!

Acrylic Paint

Use acrylic craft paint and a fine paintbrush (available at any craft store) to paint and add vibrant color to sections of your fabric. Once your paint is dry, you can stitch right on top of it. Just make sure your needle is sharp enough to pierce through the paint.

Colored Pencils

Use ordinary colored pencils or watercolor pencils to add a quick splash of color to your fabric. You could even use liquid watercolor paint to create a colorful, impressionistic base for your stitches.

Fabric Appliqué

Affix small pieces of colorful or patterned fabric to your hooped fabric to add interesting design, texture, dimension, and color to your embroidery pieces. You just need a sharp pair of scissors, a few sewing pins, and simple backstitches to open your eyes to the world of appliqué!

Beads

Beads and sequins can be stitched onto your fabric to add a little bit of sparkle and shine to your work. Take a walk through the beading aisle at your local craft store to see what catches your attention. You can incorporate beads as you please to add color and sparkle to the designs in this book!

Transferring Your Pattern

Once you've chosen your fabric, you'll need to transfer a pattern onto it. The patterns for the projects in this book start on page 152. Use one of the methods below to transfer a pattern onto your fabric.

Tracing

Use your preferred fabric transfer pen to trace the design onto your fabric. You can tape the pattern to a sunny window, tape the fabric on top, and then trace the design. This method is easy and cost effective!

You can also use a light table or create a makeshift one using your phone's flashlight and a clear tote lid. My preferred method is a makeshift light table with a heat-erasable pen, pictured at the right.

To make the pattern easier to see behind the fabric, especially if your fabric is dark, go over the lines of the pattern with a dark, fine-tipped marker before tracing.

Transfer Paper

Carbon transfer paper works really well when you're using dark or thick fabrics that you can't see through to trace a pattern. To transfer a pattern using carbon paper, layer the pieces together with your fabric on the bottom, then the transfer paper, then the pattern on top.

Use a stylus or ballpoint pen to trace over the pattern. The pressure will transfer the pattern lines onto your fabric. If the transfer is light, use a transfer pen to touch up the lines so you can clearly see where to stitch. This is my preferred method for transferring patterns onto dark fabric.

Fabric Stabilizer

These paper or fabric sheets are also sold at your local craft store. To use this method, you'll transfer the pattern onto the stabilizer, then attach the stabilizer to your hooped fabric following the package instructions provided. You stitch right on top of the stabilizer and then remove the excess when you're finished.

Step-by-Step: Tracing Your Pattern

STEP 1: Trim the fabric. Cut a square of fabric slightly larger than your chosen pattern. I like to leave 2" of extra fabric on all sides of the design. Iron out any wrinkles. Note: If you use two layers of fabric for stitching, you need to transfer your pattern only onto the top layer.

STEP 2: Choose your light source. Using tape, secure your pattern over a light source. I like to create a makeshift light table with my phone's flashlight and a tote lid. Center your fabric over the pattern. Choose a tracing pen.

STEP 3: Trace. Take your time and trace the pattern carefully. Once you finish, remove your fabric from the light source and make any necessary touch-ups with your transfer pen.

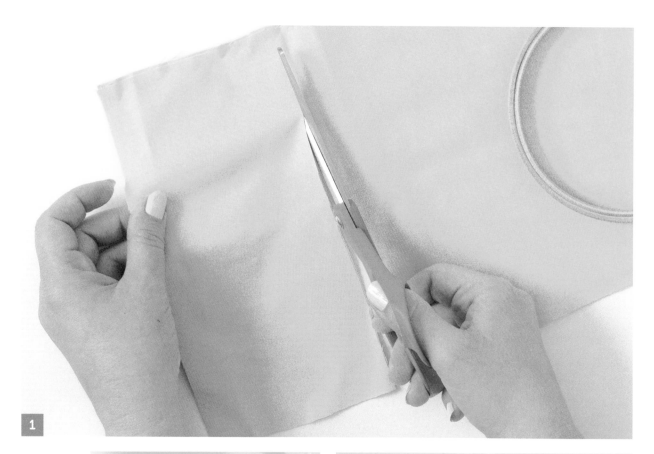

Setting Your Hoop

After you've transferred your pattern to the fabric, you'll secure the fabric in an appropriately sized embroidery hoop. Use the size listed at the beginning of the project to choose a wooden or plastic hoop that nicely frames the design. You'll need a clean, flat surface like a desk or table to set your hoop.

Step-by-Step: Setting Your Hoop

STEP 1: Separate the hoops. Separate the inner and outer hoops by unscrewing the tightening mechanism and pulling the hoops apart.

STEP 2: Position the fabric. Lay your fabric on top of the inner hoop, centering the design over it. Place the outer hoop on top of your fabric.

STEP 3: Put the hoops together. Keeping the design centered neatly in the hoops, press down on the outer hoop. It will expand to fit over the inner hoop, sandwiching the fabric in between.

STEP 4: Secure the hoops. Carefully tighten the screw on the outer hoop to hold the hoops in place.

STEP 5: Pull the fabric tight. Work your way around the hoop, gently pulling the fabric taut around the edges every quarter turn. Be sure to keep the design centered in the hoop.

STEP 6: Check the fabric. Take your time and be sure the fabric is centered, pucker and wrinkle-free, and taut. Your fabric should be drum-tight, meaning it will sound like a drum when you tap it with your fingers.

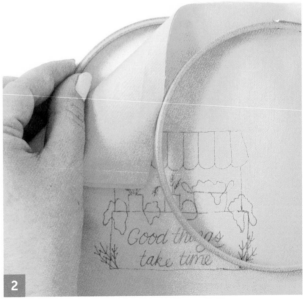

Stitching

Embroidery floss is made up of six strands. You can vary the number of strands you use to stitch your design to create different looks. When you're stitching the projects in this book, the instructions will note the number of strands needed for each element in the design. Now that you've set your hoop, it's time to separate the number of strands you need from your embroidery floss skein, thread your needle, and start stitching.

Step-by-Step: Separating the Floss

STEP 1: **Cut the floss.** Cut a length of floss about 12" to 18" long.

STEP 2: **Separate the strands.** At one end of the floss, use your fingers to separate one strand from the rest.

TIP: Always pull the floss from the numbered end of the skein to avoid a tangle.

STEP 3: **Pull.** Pull on the single strand with one hand while you hold the rest of the floss in place with the other hand. Once the strand is separated completely, set it aside.

STEP 4: **Repeat.** Repeat until you have as many strands as you need for your design. Lay them together.

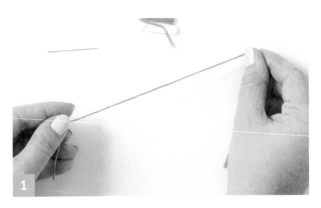

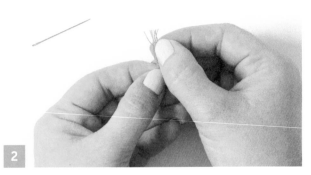

Step-by-Step: Start Stitching

STEP 1: Thread the needle. Hold your embroidery needle in one hand. In your other hand, hold the very end of the floss strands between your thumb and index finger. It may help to lightly dampen the floss. Press the eye of the needle over the end of the floss and pull a few inches of floss thorough the needle. (You can also use a needle threader instead.)

STEP 2: Secure the thread. Tie a single knot at the other end of the length of floss, about ¼" from the end.

STEP 3: Bring the needle to the front. Starting with the needle behind the fabric, push it through to the front, pulling the floss with it. The knot you made in step 2 will secure the end of your floss at the back of the fabric.

STEP 4: Practice stitching. Now you're ready to stitch away! Try a few up-and-down straight stitches to get the feel of embroidery. Make the Sunny Sampler project on page 30 to practice your stitches.

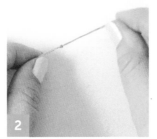

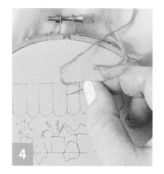

Step-by-Step: Finish Stitching

STEP 1: Trim the floss. When you've finished stitching, are nearing the end of the floss, or want to switch colors, bring the floss to the back of the fabric and trim it, leaving a 2" tail.

STEP 2: Tie the floss. Split the strands of floss into two evenly sized bundles and tightly tie them into a knot against the fabric.

STEP 3: Finish. Trim the floss tails to about ¼" long.

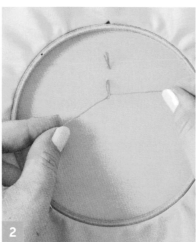
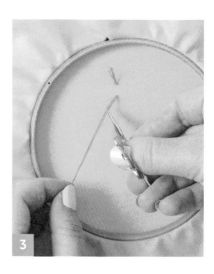

Finishing the Back of Your Hoop

After you've completed a piece of embroidery, it's time to finish it so you can display it. Traditionally, the back of a hoop is stitched closed with a running stitch. This pulls together all the excess fabric, gathering it at the back. Then, this is covered with a circle of felt stitched to the excess fabric. Alternatively, you can use the quick gluing method outlined on the next page with a fabric-safe glue. Either way, before you finish the back of your hoop, there are a few final steps to complete.

Finishing Touches

- Ensure your stitching is completely finished—if you use glue to close the back of the hoop, you won't be able to make edits to the piece later.

- Trim any excess floss tails on the back.

- Remove any remaining transfer pen marks according to your pen's packaging instructions.

- Gently tighten the fabric and check the tension of the hoop's screw.

Step-by-Step: Finishing the Back

STEP 1: Cut the circle. Take an embroidery hoop that's the same size as your finished project and trace the inner hoop on cardstock. Cut out the circle.

STEP 2: Trim the fabric. Trim the excess fabric at the back of the hoop, leaving about 1" around the edges.

STEP 3: Add the circle. Place the cardstock circle in the hoop against the back of your stitches.

STEP 4: Glue. Add a thin ring of fabric-safe glue around the edge of the cardstock circle and the back of the inner hoop.

STEP 5: Secure the fabric. Fold the fabric over the edge of the inner hoop and firmly press it in place on the cardstock until it sticks.

STEP 6: Repeat as needed. If you stitched your design on multiple layers of fabric, repeat steps 4 and 5 with the second layer of fabric.

Now your hoop is ready to be displayed! Use a small finishing nail, pushpin, or even a bit of twine and colorful washi tape to hang your hoop on the wall. Your finished piece could also rest on a mantle or bookshelf.

TIP: Before adding the circle to the back of your hoop, sign and date it, or, if you're gifting the piece, inscribe a message for the hoop's recipient on it.

Wear It or Share It

Once you get comfortable with embroidery, I think you'll have a lot of fun thinking outside the hoop and dreaming up projects to wear or share. You can add embroidery to clothing, accessories, and pieces of home décor like linen napkins, decorative banners, or pillows, among many other keepsakes and textiles.

Adding embroidery to your clothing by stitching directly on it or by creating a wearable patch can make such a cool and personal statement. Use any of the patterns in this book, or combine small elements from them, to create just the right design for your garment.

When stitching on a garment like a hat, shirt, or baby blanket, there are just a few things to keep in mind.

- Wash the fabric to preshrink it so it doesn't warp or distort your stitching when you wash it later.

- Use a stabilizer to reinforce your stitching, especially if you're working on fabric with a little stretch.

- Use a hoop to keep your work surface pulled taut.

- Keep your stitches very short, no longer than ¼", to avoid loose, pulled stitches.

- Once your stitching is complete, handwash your garment as needed to protect the delicate embroidery.

Split backstitch and long and short stitch make excellent fill stitches for adding my patterns to clothing. These short, taut stitches are less likely to be pulled out with wear. I used the poppy pattern from the Wildflower Study project on page 64 and the adorable orange from the Summer Citrus project on page 98 to customize these linen overalls and canvas tote.

This linen sleeveless top and mustard bandana got a makeover with my Wildflower Study project on page 64.

If you want a quick project to practice stitching on garments, take a look at the little megaphones in the Say It Loud project on page 38. You can see I'm using sticky stabilizer paper to mark the pattern on my shirt. This type of stabilizer washes away with water.

Sunny Sampler

Are you ready to practice some stitches? This Sunny Sampler, based on my favorite weekend activities, will help you get acquainted with the fifteen embroidery stitches used to create the projects in this book. Use the pattern on page 33 and the Embroidery Stitch Library on page 144, settle in, and get cozy! You can use any fabric and floss colors that make you happy to create this design.

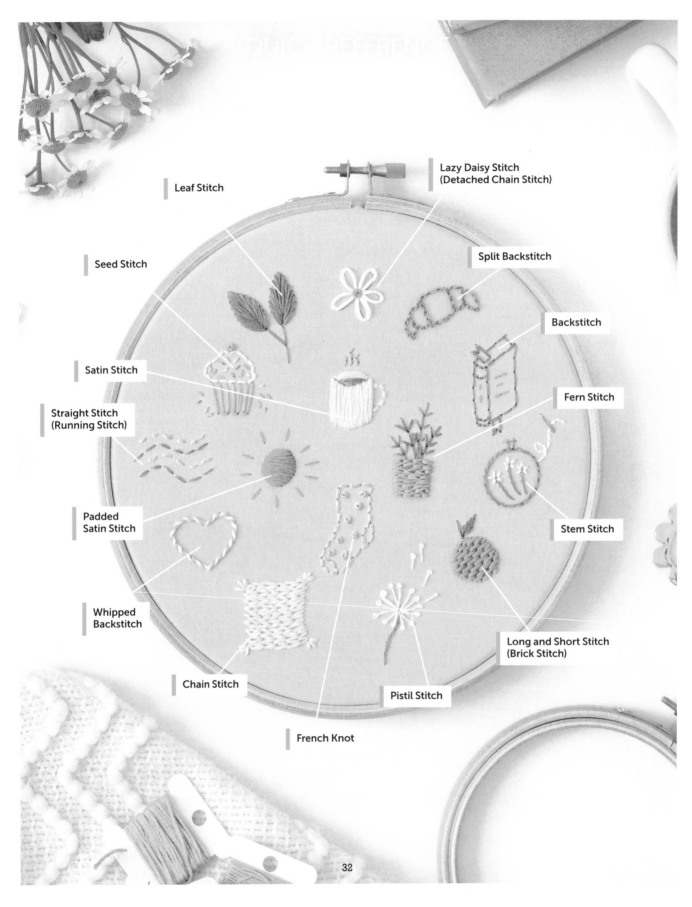

Leaf Stitch

Lazy Daisy Stitch
(Detached Chain Stitch)

Seed Stitch

Split Backstitch

Backstitch

Satin Stitch

Fern Stitch

Straight Stitch
(Running Stitch)

Stem Stitch

Padded
Satin Stitch

Whipped
Backstitch

Long and Short Stitch
(Brick Stitch)

Chain Stitch

Pistil Stitch

French Knot

Sunny Sampler Pattern

The Projects

I had so much fun creating the projects in this book, and I hope you'll have just as much fun stitching them. As you prepare to stitch a design, don't forget—embroidery is an opportunity to express your creativity! Follow the patterns and colors exactly or let your imagination run wild. No matter what, have fun!

36

Rise & Shine

*Write it on your heart that every day
is the best day in the year.*
RALPH WALDO EMERSON

Hello, sunshine! I'm so glad you're here! With this first set of patterns, we're going to focus on starting our days off the right way. What rituals help you begin your day on the sunny side? Coffee, a nourishing breakfast, meditation, quiet time, prayer, or daily affirmations? Maybe a sunrise walk or a skincare routine? Whatever it is, I encourage you to take the time each day to invest in caring for yourself, setting intentions for your day, and enjoying the life you have!

Are you an early bird? It's taken me several years to realize that I am actually a certified morning person, and I delighted in creating these early-morning-inspired projects for you. They're all suitable for beginners, so this is a very good place for anyone to start! Pour yourself a cup of coffee (or two or three), find a sunny spot, and let's start stitching!

Jot down three daily affirmations that you need to hear from yourself each morning. Or list the daily rituals that help you begin your day on the sunny side. What is a new habit or two that you'd like to add to that list?

Say It Loud

STITCHES

- Backstitch
- Straight stitch

SUPPLIES

- 4" embroidery hoop
- 7" x 7" piece of your chosen fabric
- 1 skein of your chosen floss
- Embroidery scissors
- Embroidery needle
- Transfer materials (page 20)
- Finishing materials (page 26)
- Pattern (page 153)

We could all use a little encouragement and inspiration to help us begin our day! Do you have daily affirmations that inspire you each morning? Peace, love, and coffee? Or perhaps: Be Kind, Be Brave, and Be You? I've included a few words for this project that I thought you might want to stitch as a starting point, but you get to make this your own!

If you're brand new to the world of embroidery, this is an excellent project for you because of its simplicity. You need to know only the two most basic embroidery stitches, and you only need one color of floss. I recommend choosing a simple cotton or linen for your fabric and one color of highly contrasting floss to make sure your words stand out. I used a mustard linen with white cotton embroidery floss, but feel free to get creative with your fabric and floss color combinations. ■

TIP: A note about knots: As you stitch, you'll inevitably encounter pesky knots. Working slowly with short lengths of floss (18" long or less) will help you keep knots to a minimum. As you pull the floss through the tightly stretched fabric, it will become twisted and strained. Periodically, stop stitching and let your needle hang down from your hoop so the floss can unwind. Then you can start stitching again. If you notice a knot forming as you pull the floss through the fabric, stop as soon as you see it and gently use your needle to pull on the strands and untangle it.

Shout Lines
White | Straight stitch | 6 strands

Megaphone Outline
White | Backstitch | 6 strands

Megaphone Details
White | Backstitch | 6 strands

Text
White | Backstitch | 6 strands

TIP: Once you feel comfortable with your stitching skills, try adding your own words to the megaphone pattern. Choose any word, phrase, or daily affirmation you like and write it on your fabric. Or, if you wish, use a computer to print the text and trace it onto your fabric.

STEP 1: Prepare your materials. Following the tutorials in the Getting Started section, transfer your pattern, set your hoop, and separate your floss. Thread your needle with six strands.

STEP 2: Start the megaphone outline. Make a ¼" stitch along the megaphone outline, ending with the needle behind the fabric. Bring the needle up through the fabric ¼" from your first stitch. Stitch backward, pushing your needle through the hole at the end of your first stitch. Your stitches will be touching and sharing the same hole in the fabric. This is called backstitch.

STEP 3: Finish the megaphone outline. Continue outlining the megaphone with backstitch. Keep your stitches equal in length as you work your way around the shape.

Say It Loud

STEP 4: Stitch the megaphone details. Using six strands of floss, outline the megaphone's handle and mouthpiece in backstitch.

STEP 5: Stitch the shout lines. Using six strands of floss, make a straight stitch over each line coming out of the megaphone. Bring the needle up at the beginning of the line, then push the needle through at the end of the line, and repeat for each line. This is called straight stitch.

STEP 6: Stitch the letters. Using six strands of floss, outline the letters in backstitch. For gently curved lines, keep your stitches slightly shorter than ¼". Short stitches make it easier to outline curves than long stitches.

STEP 7: Finish. Follow the steps on page 26 to finish the back of the hoop. Remove any transfer pen marks as needed.

TIP: This pattern makes a great statement stitched onto a T-shirt or sweatshirt! For a few tips on embroidering garments, take a look at page 28.

On the Sunny Side

STITCHES

- Padded satin stitch

SUPPLIES

- 6" embroidery hoop
- 9" x 9" piece of your chosen fabric
- 1 skein of mustard floss
- Embroidery scissors
- Embroidery needle
- White acrylic craft paint
- Small paintbrush
- Transfer materials (page 20)
- Finishing materials (page 26)
- Pattern (page 154)

I think there isn't a more cheerful way to start your day than with a plate of sunny-side-up eggs! While these embroidered eggs won't give you the nutrition the OG superfood provides, they'll look absolutely adorable hanging in your kitchen or stitched on a throw pillow for your home. And I think you'll really enjoy painting and stitching them!

Unsure about the acrylic craft paint? Keep reading! Yes, this project uses paint, which is not a supply you'd expect to see in an embroidery book! But I encourage you to give it a chance and see how much fun it is to add a bit of color to your fabric before stitching. Once the paint dries completely, you can stitch over it. Incorporating this additional medium can take your embroidery to a new level and create so much color, texture, and visual interest! You can find this affordable and easy-to-use paint in little bottles or tubes at your local craft store. If you prefer to keep paint out of the mix, simply use a fill stitch of your choice, like satin stitch or split backstitch, to fill in the egg whites. ■

TIP: You'll give your egg yolks a rounded, three-dimensional effect by filling them in with a base layer of floss, then using smooth satin stitches to cover the base layer. This technique is known as padded satin stitch.

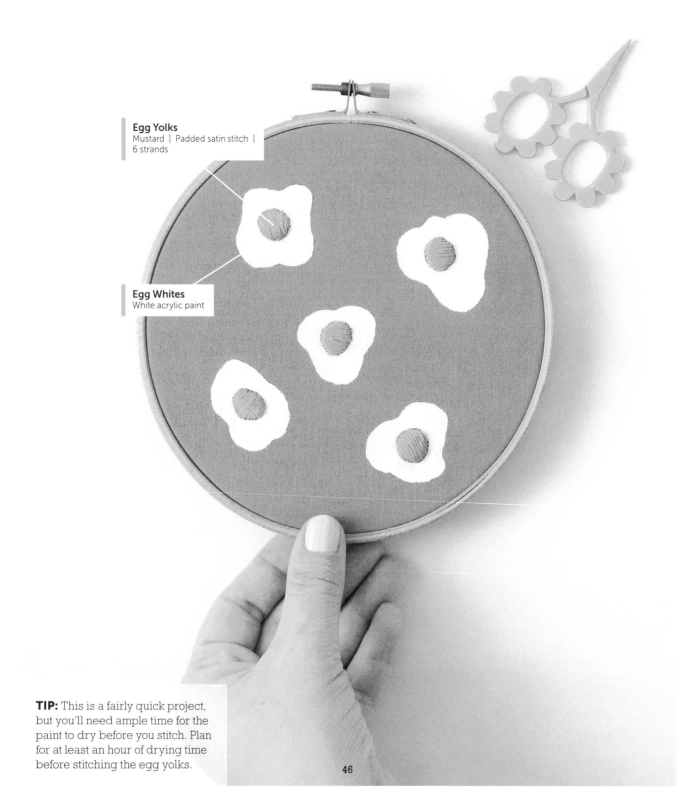

Egg Yolks
Mustard | Padded satin stitch |
6 strands

Egg Whites
White acrylic paint

TIP: This is a fairly quick project, but you'll need ample time for the paint to dry before you stitch. Plan for at least an hour of drying time before stitching the egg yolks.

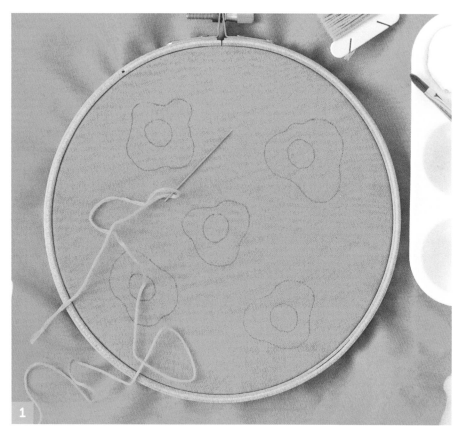

STEP 1: Prepare your materials. Following the tutorials in the Getting Started section, transfer your pattern, set your hoop, and separate your floss. Thread your needle with six strands of mustard floss. Pour a small amount of white acrylic paint onto a paint palette.

STEP 2: Paint the egg whites. Using a small paintbrush, fill in the egg white shapes with one coat of white acrylic paint. Allow the paint to dry thoroughly (for at least one hour).

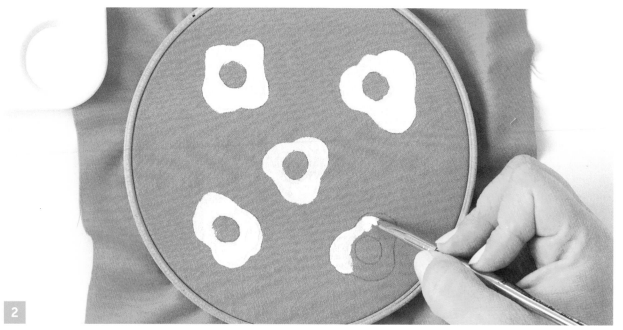

On the Sunny Side

STEP 3: Start stitching the egg yolks. Using six strands of mustard floss, fill the yolk circle of each egg with compact, parallel satin stitches. Start the stitch at one side of the circle and end it directly opposite on the other side, stitching across the widest part of the circle. Add another stitch parallel to the first one. Continue making close, parallel stitches until half of the circle is filled in, then repeat for the other half of the circle.

STEP 4: Finish stitching the egg yolks. Add a second layer of satin stitches to each egg yolk, stitching over the base layer you made in step 3. Make this layer of stitches perpendicular to the base layer stitches. Start at the widest part of each circle, filling in one half and then the other.

STEP 5: Finish. Follow the steps on page 26 to finish the back of the hoop. Remove any transfer pen marks as needed.

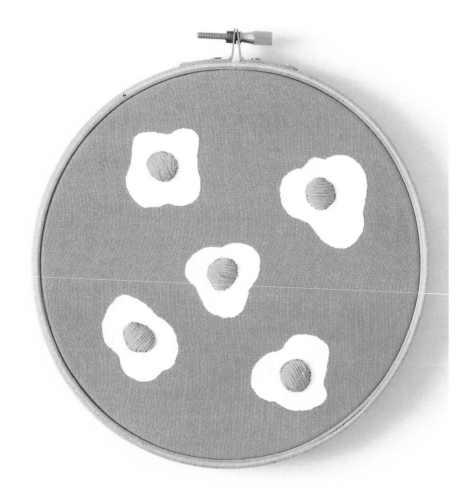

You Got This

STITCHES

- Backstitch
- Seed stitch

SUPPLIES

- 4" embroidery hoop
- 7" x 7" piece of your chosen fabric
- 1 skein each of red, orange, yellow, bright-green, teal, pink, and white floss
- Embroidery scissors
- Embroidery needle
- Transfer materials (page 20)
- Finishing materials (page 26)
- Pattern (page 155)

What makes you feel like you can do almost anything? For me, it's support and encouragement from the people in my life I love the most. But sometimes, sugar (especially in the form of a pink sprinkled donut) motivates me. This project incorporates both!

Two simple stitches make up this pattern, and you already know them! The text is backstitch, a simple, effective stitch for outlining almost anything in embroidery. We'll make the sprinkles on this piece by scattering short straight stitches all around randomly, also known as seed stitch. Seed stitch allows us to fill in large fabric sections quickly and with a whimsical flair. Because of the simplicity of this project, it's a great one for beginners to start with. DONUT worry; you got this! ■

TIP: As you work, take note of your posture. Pay attention to signs that your neck, back, or hands need a rest. Embroidery can be so fun and utterly captivating that you may not notice the hours passing by! It may be helpful to set a timer as a reminder to stand up, stretch, and check on your needs. You are important, so please remember to take care of yourself!

Text
Red | Backstitch | 6 strands

YOU
GOT
THIS

Sprinkles
Red, orange, yellow, bright
green, teal, pink, white |
Seed stitch | 6 strands

TIP: You can change the look of this design by
using a color scheme of your choosing. I chose
bright rainbow sprinkles, but a boho neutral
color scheme would also look great. Try using
cream-colored fabric, tan lettering, and rust,
mustard, and brown shades for the sprinkles!

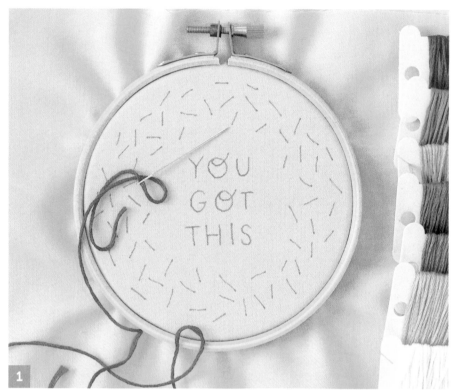

STEP 1: Prepare your materials. Following the tutorials in the Getting Started section, transfer your pattern, set your hoop, and separate your floss. Thread your needle with six strands of red floss.

STEP 2: Stitch the letters. Using six strands of red floss, outline the letters in backstitch. For a uniform look, keep your stitches very short and make each one the same length.

53

You Got This

STEP 3: Start stitching the sprinkles. Using six strands of red floss, make a straight stitch over one of the sprinkles in the pattern. Make another stitch, spacing it away from the first one. Repeat, scattering red straight stitches throughout the pattern. You can assign colors to each sprinkle at random or use my sample photo as a reference.

STEP 4: Finish stitching the sprinkles. Repeat step 3 with each remaining floss color (orange, yellow, bright green, teal, pink, and white).

STEP 5: Finish. Follow the steps on page 26 to finish the hoop. Remove any transfer pen marks as needed.

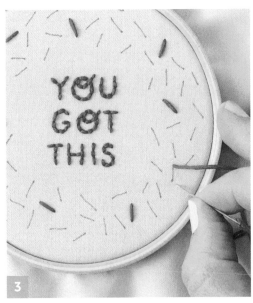

Shine Bright

STITCHES

- Split backstitch
- Seed stitch
- Satin stitch
- French knot

SUPPLIES

- 6" embroidery hoop
- 9" x 9" piece of your chosen fabric
- 1 skein each of mustard, light-green, pale-aqua, burnt-orange, baby-pink, carnation-pink, and lavender floss
- Embroidery scissors
- Embroidery needle
- Transfer materials (page 20)
- Finishing materials (page 26)
- Pattern (page 156)

I have heard it said that embroidery can be a meditative art, and I think this piece lends itself to that exceptionally well. Take your time and enjoy filling in each shape of this design with purpose and care. Notice the way the light catches the strands of your embroidery floss, and enjoy feeling its texture with your hands. Follow along with the color scheme I used, or choose colors from your floss collection that draw you in. This is a time-consuming project, so don't worry about how long or how many stitching sessions it takes. You may want to develop a daily practice to cultivate mindfulness, filling in one section each day until the project is complete. There's no wrong way to stitch this sunrise!

While you work on this piece, I want you to know that the world needs your beautiful light! What you have to offer this world is unique, meaningful, and irreplaceable. Let this sunrise be a reminder to you to bring brightness to the world whenever you can! ■

TIP: To make your satin stitches neat and tidy, separate your floss into two or three bundles. Then put six strands together again before threading your needle. This makes the floss more uniform and helps it lie flat.

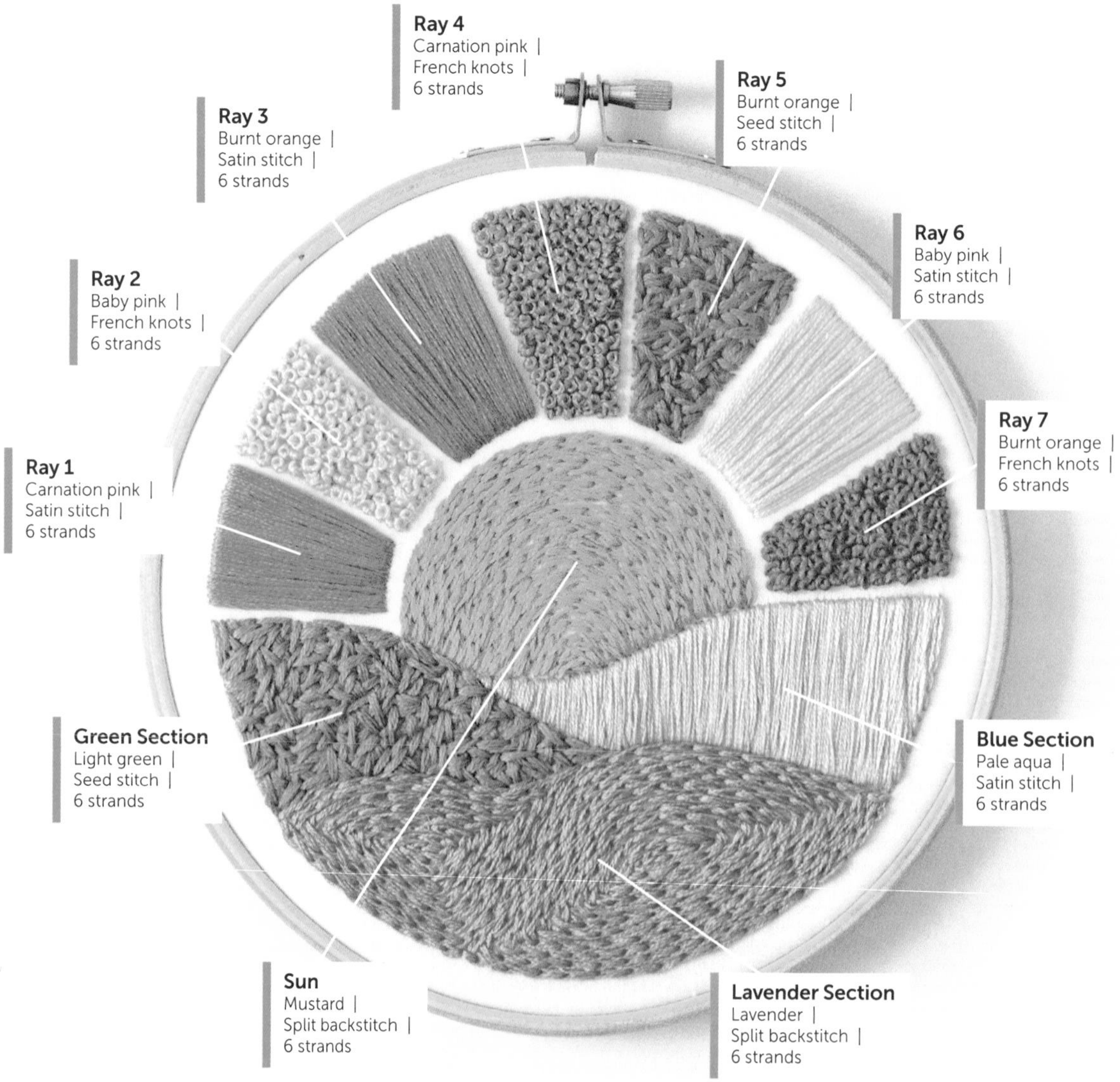

Ray 4
Carnation pink |
French knots |
6 strands

Ray 5
Burnt orange |
Seed stitch |
6 strands

Ray 3
Burnt orange |
Satin stitch |
6 strands

Ray 6
Baby pink |
Satin stitch |
6 strands

Ray 2
Baby pink |
French knots |
6 strands

Ray 7
Burnt orange |
French knots |
6 strands

Ray 1
Carnation pink |
Satin stitch |
6 strands

Green Section
Light green |
Seed stitch |
6 strands

Blue Section
Pale aqua |
Satin stitch |
6 strands

Sun
Mustard |
Split backstitch |
6 strands

Lavender Section
Lavender |
Split backstitch |
6 strands

TIP: Trace the guidelines in the pattern—they will help you fill in the shapes. Satin stitch can be especially tricky when you're working in large sections. Dividing a shape into smaller parts can help you keep your stitches parallel to one another. The guidelines in the shapes filled with split backstitch will help direct your stitches to create a sense of movement.

58

STEP 1: Prepare your materials. Following the tutorials in the Getting Started section, transfer your pattern, set your hoop, and separate your floss. Thread your needle with six strands of mustard floss.

STEP 2: Fill in the sun. Using six strands of mustard floss, fill in the sun with split backstitch. Starting along the edge of the sun, make a ¼" straight stitch. Bring your needle up about ¼" away from the end of the first stitch. Stitch backward, pushing your needle through the middle of the first stitch, splitting the six strands of floss in half. Continue making split backstitches along the edge of the sun. Then, add additional rows of split backstitch to fill the center. The pattern guidelines will help you keep your rows neat and aligned.

STEP 3: Fill in Ray 1. Using six strands of carnation pink, sati-stitch the first sunray. Start each stitch at the top of the ray and stitch down toward the sun. Overlap or make some of the stitches shorter so you'll have enough room where the ray narrows. This is an artful technique, and it may take a little trial and error to get your stitches to fit just right.

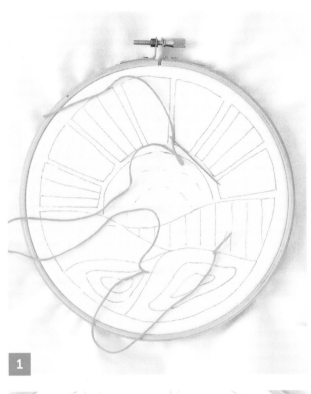

1

2

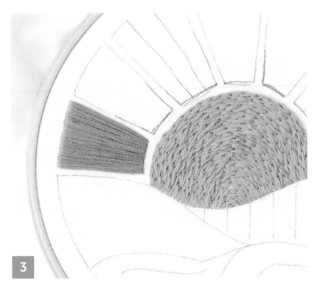

3

Shine Bright

STEP 4: Fill in Ray 2. Using six strands of baby-pink floss, fill in the second ray with densely spaced French knots (see page 145 for a detailed tutorial). When forming the knots, wrap the thread around your needle once or twice, depending on the size of knot you prefer.

STEP 5: Fill in Ray 3. Using six strands of burnt-orange floss, satin-stitch the third ray.

STEP 6: Fill in Ray 4. Using six strands of carnation pink, fill in the fourth ray with French knots.

STEP 7: Fill in Ray 5. Using six strands of burnt-orange floss, fill in the fifth ray with seed stitches.

Make your stitches equal in length (about ¼" each) and place them randomly within the ray. You can determine how much of your fabric shows through by how densely you place the stitches. Add multiple layers, crossing stitches over one another to cover the fabric.

STEP 8: Fill in Ray 6. Using six strands of baby-pink floss, fill in the sixth ray with satin stitch.

STEP 9: Fill in Ray 7. Using six strands of burnt-orange floss, fill in the seventh ray with French knots.

STEP 10: Fill in the blue section. Using six strands of pale-aqua floss, satin-stitch the area below the

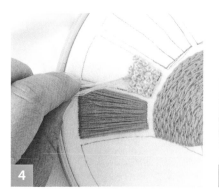
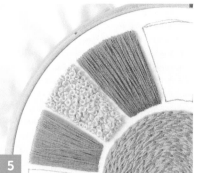
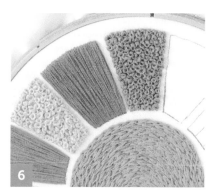
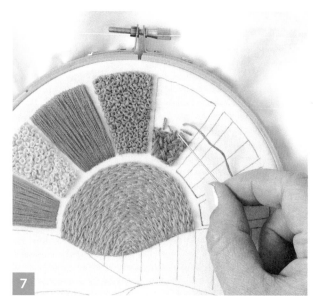
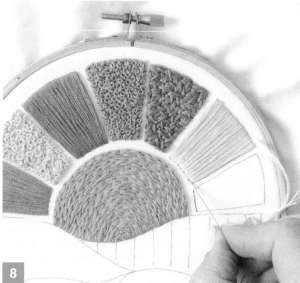

right side of the sun. Make vertical stitches (running from top to bottom in the shape) and keep them compact to completely cover the fabric. Use the guidelines and work on small sections at a time until you've filled in the entire shape.

STEP 11: **Fill in the green section.** Using six strands of light-green floss, fill in the area below the left side of the sun with densely spaced seed stitches.

STEP 12: **Fill in the bottom section.** Using six strands of lavender floss, fill in the shape at the bottom of the design with split backstitch. To help keep your stitches in line, work on the shape in two sections, following the guidelines on the pattern. Begin by outlining a section with a row of split backstitch, then continue adding rows of split backstitch following the contours of the outline to fill the center.

STEP 13: **Finish.** Follow the steps on page 26 to finish the hoop. Remove any transfer pen marks as needed.

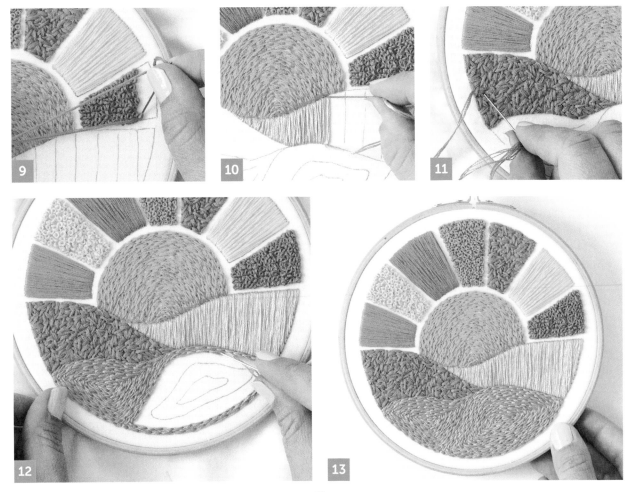

Play in the Garden

*It was June, and the world smelled of roses. The sunshine
was like powdered gold over the grassy hillside.*
MAUD HART LOVELACE

When was the last time you stopped to smell the daisies
(or the roses)? Or worked with your hands in the garden?
Or spent time resting or playing surrounded by nature?
There is something truly therapeutic about growing flowers,
vegetables, berries, and herbs on your own.

Spending the day in a garden, whether your own, a local
greenhouse, or a city botanical garden, can bring peace
to your heart and encourage you to slow down and take in
the abundant beauty of nature with a childlike wonder.
By taking precious time to plan, plant, care for, and play
in a garden, we can come to the realization that sunny days
are always ahead. The bright botanical patterns
in this section reflect that sentiment.

**What are some of your childhood memories of
exploring nature in the summertime?**

Wildflower Study

STITCHES

- Backstitch
- Straight stitch

SUPPLIES

- Three 4" embroidery hoops
- Three 7" x 7" pieces of your chosen fabric
- 1 skein of white floss
- Embroidery scissors
- Embroidery needle
- Transfer materials (page 20)
- Finishing materials (page 26)
- Pattern (page 157)

We are so lucky to live in a world where wildflowers grow! The vibrant colors, rich texture, and remarkable variety make a wildflower patch completely captivating. Whether grown in your backyard or thriving naturally in a meadow or along a highway, wildflowers provide an essential food source for local fauna and play a pivotal role in sustaining the pollinator population.

Where I live in Texas, we look forward to different varieties of wildflowers in the spring (hello, beautiful bluebonnets!), summer, fall, and even the winter. But this trio of wildflowers, featuring coneflowers, poppies, and buttercups, can brighten your day and remind you of the charming beauty of nature, no matter what season it is or where you live.

You can follow my lead on this project and outline the flowers with backstitch. Or, if you're ready for a more advanced project, fill in the flower petals with your choice of colors and fill stitches, like satin or split backstitch. These simple designs would look great stitched on a T-shirt pocket, tea towels, or linen napkins for a special gift. ■

TIP: Remember that your stitches don't have to be permanent. Anytime you encounter a problem while you're stitching, you can stop, carefully snip the stitches with your embroidery scissors (avoiding the fabric), pull out the floss, and start again with a new length of floss. Embroidery is a very forgiving craft, and learning from your mistakes and mishaps is part of the process.

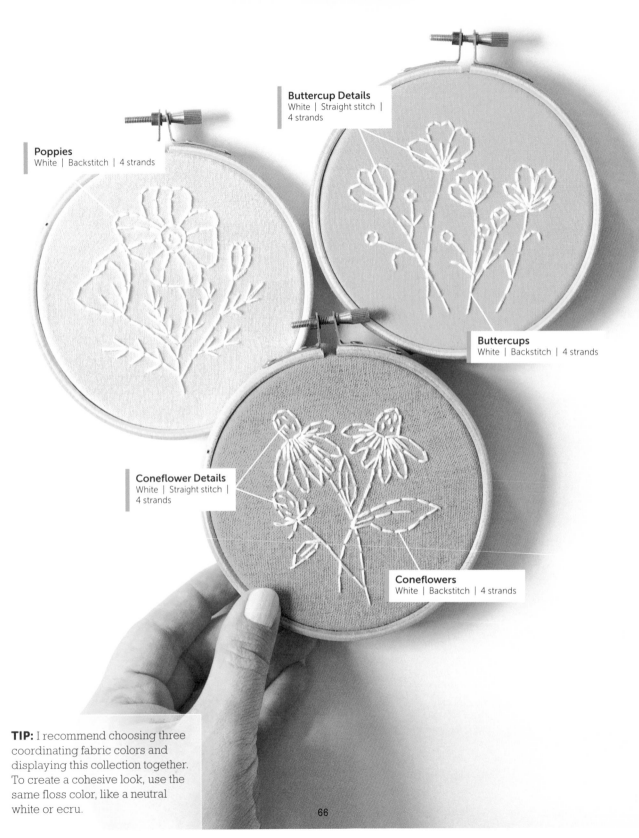

Poppies
White | Backstitch | 4 strands

Buttercup Details
White | Straight stitch | 4 strands

Buttercups
White | Backstitch | 4 strands

Coneflower Details
White | Straight stitch | 4 strands

Coneflowers
White | Backstitch | 4 strands

TIP: I recommend choosing three coordinating fabric colors and displaying this collection together. To create a cohesive look, use the same floss color, like a neutral white or ecru.

66

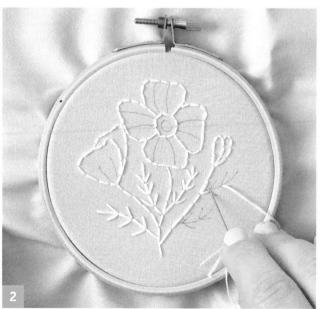

STEP 1: Prepare your materials. Following the tutorials in the Getting Started section, transfer your patterns, set your hoops, and separate your floss. Thread your needle with four strands of white floss.

STEP 2: Stitch the poppies. Using four strands of white floss, outline the poppy petals, stems, bud, and leaves with ¼" backstitch. Then, add the details to the flower petals with backstitch.

Wildflower Study

STEP 3: Stitch the coneflowers. Using four strands of white floss, outline the coneflower petals, centers, stems, and leaves with ¼" backstitch. Then, make straight stitches to add the details to the coneflowers' centers.

STEP 4: Stitch the buttercups. Using four strands of white floss, outline the buttercup petals, buds, stems, and leaves with ¼" backstitches. Then, make straight stitches to add the details to the buttercups' petals.

STEP 5: Finish. Follow the steps on page 26 to finish each hoop. Remove any transfer pen marks as needed.

Sunny Days Ahead

STITCHES

- Backstitch
- French knot
- Satin stitch
- Stem stitch
- Whipped backstitch
- Leaf stitch
- Fern stitch

SUPPLIES

- 5" embroidery hoop
- 8" x 8" piece of your chosen fabric
- 1 skein each of black, dark-brown, coral, salmon, orange, yellow, yellow-green, and bright-green floss
- Salmon colored pencil
- Embroidery scissors
- Embroidery needle
- Transfer materials (page 20)
- Finishing materials (page 26)
- Pattern (page 158)

When we plant a garden, we put our hope into knowing the sun will shine on it, sustain it, and make it bloom. Just the same, as we persevere through challenging moments and days, we know a sunny day can be just around the corner. As you stitch this, I want you to remember that whatever hard days or season you're in the thick of, take good care of yourself, hang in there, and keep looking forward.

Are you ready to try something new? You've picked the right project! You'll notice that this design uses colored pencils to add a quick wash of color to the banner. You can use any color you like, and any old colored pencils will do for this technique (I borrowed mine from my kids' craft basket!).

Do you love all things botanical and creating botanical embroidery? Then you'll want to master the stem stitch, fern stitch, and leaf stitch, all three of which are introduced in this project. I think you'll find all these techniques useful for any plant and flower embroidery you'll do inside and outside this book. ∎

TIP: Whipped backstitch is a great outline stitch and will be used to outline the banner in this project. This stitch creates a seamless outline, covering up all the floss entry points from the first layer of backstitch. This stitch has two parts, and you can use two different floss colors to make a unique, striped look. Use black for the first step (backstitch), then white for the second step (whip-stitch). The end result will resemble charming baker's twine!

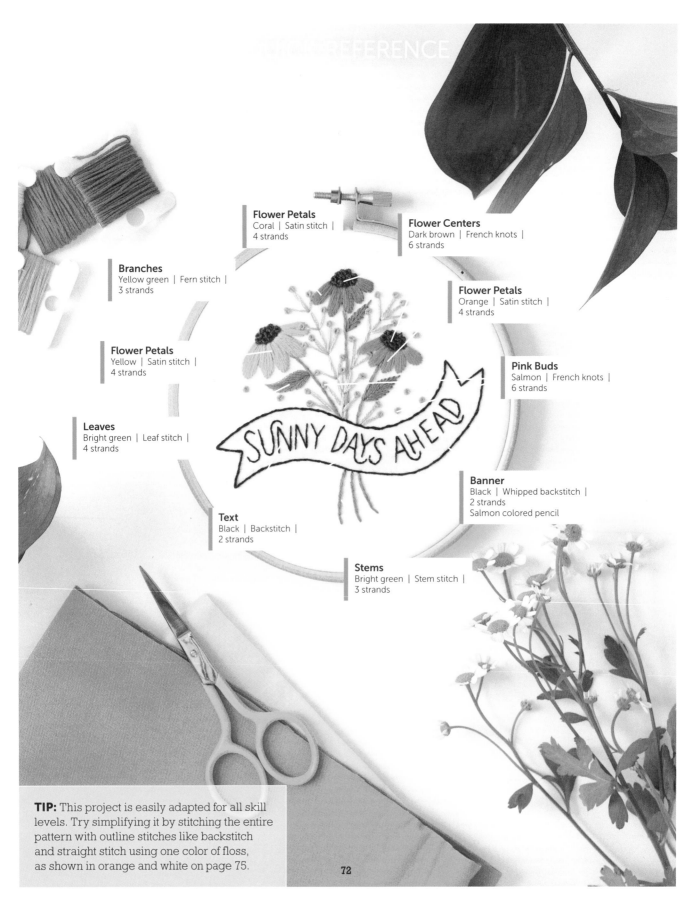

Flower Petals
Coral | Satin stitch |
4 strands

Flower Centers
Dark brown | French knots |
6 strands

Branches
Yellow green | Fern stitch |
3 strands

Flower Petals
Orange | Satin stitch |
4 strands

Flower Petals
Yellow | Satin stitch |
4 strands

Pink Buds
Salmon | French knots |
6 strands

Leaves
Bright green | Leaf stitch |
4 strands

Banner
Black | Whipped backstitch |
2 strands
Salmon colored pencil

Text
Black | Backstitch |
2 strands

Stems
Bright green | Stem stitch |
3 strands

TIP: This project is easily adapted for all skill levels. Try simplifying it by stitching the entire pattern with outline stitches like backstitch and straight stitch using one color of floss, as shown in orange and white on page 75.

72

STEP 1: Prepare your materials. Following the tutorials in the Getting Started section, transfer your pattern, set your hoop, and separate your floss. Thread your needle with two strands of black floss. Choose a salmon or pink colored pencil.

STEP 2: Color the banner. Color in the banner with the colored pencil. Use steady, gentle strokes to give the banner an even, colorful fill.

STEP 3: Start outlining the banner. Using two strands of black floss, outline the banner with backstitch.

Sunny Days Ahead

STEP 4: Finish outlining the banner. Now it's time to complete the whipped backstitch. Using two strands of black floss, bring your needle to the front of the fabric at the bottom left corner of the banner. Guide the needle under the thread of the first backstitch. Bring your needle over the first backstitch and guide it under the second backstitch. Repeat, pulling the floss gently as you wrap it around each backstitch you made in step 3. When you reach a corner, bring your needle to the back of the fabric to secure the thread, and start again on the next straight edge. Continue until you have stitched along the entire outline, then bring your needle to the back of the fabric at the starting point.

STEP 5: Stitch the text. Using two strands of black floss, outline the letters in backstitch. Keep your stitches uniform in length and make them short so you can closely follow the letters' contours.

STEP 6: Stitch the flower stems. Using three strands of bright-green floss, outline the flower stems in stem stitch. Make a ¼" stitch along a stem line, but don't pull the thread all the way through. Instead, gently hold the thread to the side, making a small arch. Bring your needle up between the ends of the arch. Now pull the thread taut, making the arch flat. Make another straight stitch, holding the thread to the side to make a small arch. Bring your needle up between the ends of the arch, using the same hole as the end of the arch from the first stitch.

STEP 7: Stitch the leaves. Using four strands of bright-green floss, fill in the leaves with leaf stitch. Start with one straight stitch down the center of the leaf. Make it from the leaf's tip to about three-quarters of the way to the base. Start the second stitch by bringing the needle out on the top left side of the first stitch at the edge of the leaf. Cross over

the first stitch, ending just to its right in the middle of the leaf. Repeat on the opposite side of the leaf. Continue stitching to the base of the leaf, keeping your stitches parallel to one another on each side.

STEP 8: **Stitch the flower petals.** Using four strands of yellow floss, fill in a flower with satin stitch. Start at the tip of each petal and end at the flower's center, keeping the stitches compact and equal in length. Repeat with the coral and orange floss to fill the remaining flowers.

STEP 9: **Stitch the flower centers.** Using six strands of dark-brown floss, fill the flower centers with compact French knots (about ten per flower center). Wrap the floss around your needle one to two times for each knot.

STEP 10: **Stitch the flower branches.** Using three strands of yellow-green floss, outline the branches with fern stitch. Backstitch along the main branch, then add short straight stitches for the twigs where the backstitches meet.

STEP 11: **Stitch the flower buds.** Using six strands of salmon floss, make a French knot at the end of each twig. Wrap the floss around your needle one to two times to make small, tidy flower buds. Finally, add a French knot wherever a dot is shown on the pattern.

STEP 12: **Finish.** Follow the steps on page 26 to finish the hoop. Remove any transfer pen marks as needed.

Miniature Greenhouse

STITCHES

- Backstitch
- Straight stitch
- Fern stitch
- Satin stitch
- Leaf stitch

SUPPLIES

- 4" embroidery hoop
- 7" x 7" piece of your chosen fabric
- 1 skein each of mustard, black, light-jade, bright-green, forest-green, and yellow-green floss
- Embroidery scissors
- Embroidery needle
- Transfer materials (page 20)
- Finishing materials (page 26)
- Pattern (page 159)

One of my favorite things to do on a Saturday morning is walk through the warm and sunny greenhouse at my local plant nursery, admiring all the plants. (This requires a lot of restraint because I really don't have the space for any more plants!) One of my dreams is to have a small greenhouse of my own in my backyard. Wouldn't it be great to provide a cozy space for seedlings and plants to grow year-round? And as a bonus, it sounds like the perfect little retreat away from the real world! Caring for plants, learning their needs, and nurturing them is a hobby that grounds me and gives me peace.

Are you a plant person, too? Even if you're not, this miniature greenhouse will add some low-maintenance greenery to your space that needs no care from you at all. You'll be using simple stitches that have all been covered in the book thus far, but on a much-smaller scale. This pocket-sized greenhouse looks great displayed in a hoop, stitched on a canvas pouch, or added to the pocket of a comfy shirt. ■

TIP: Working on such a small-scale design can be a challenge, so set yourself up for success by having a great light source and a sharp needle, and consider using a craft magnifier if your eyesight is strained. I like to clamp a small book light onto the edge of my hoop to give me adequate light if I'm stitching at night. Remember to take good care of yourself as you enjoy your crafty hobbies!

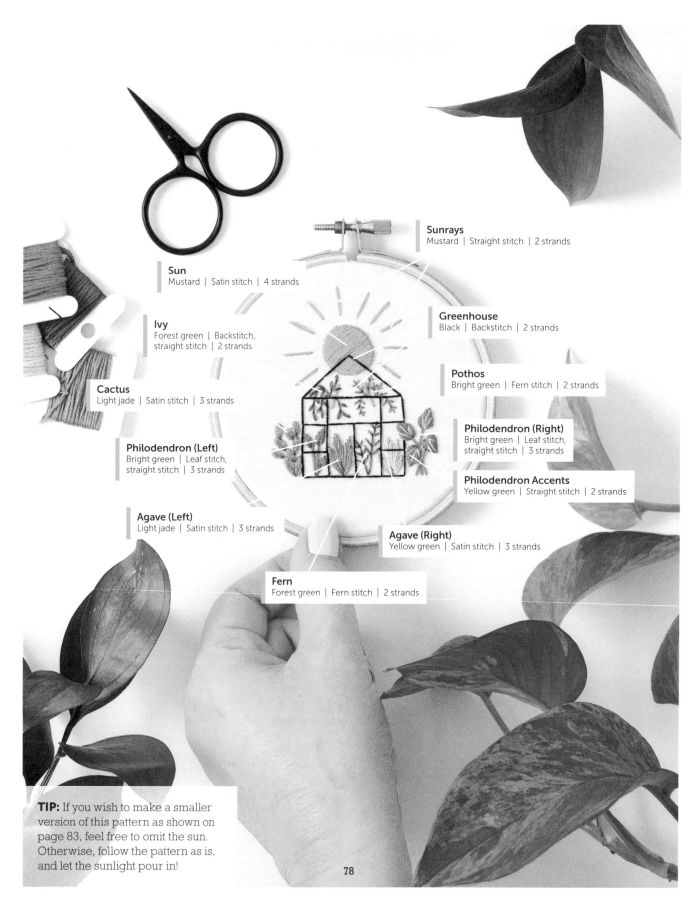

Sun
Mustard | Satin stitch | 4 strands

Sunrays
Mustard | Straight stitch | 2 strands

Ivy
Forest green | Backstitch, straight stitch | 2 strands

Greenhouse
Black | Backstitch | 2 strands

Pothos
Bright green | Fern stitch | 2 strands

Cactus
Light jade | Satin stitch | 3 strands

Philodendron (Left)
Bright green | Leaf stitch, straight stitch | 3 strands

Philodendron (Right)
Bright green | Leaf stitch, straight stitch | 3 strands

Philodendron Accents
Yellow green | Straight stitch | 2 strands

Agave (Left)
Light jade | Satin stitch | 3 strands

Agave (Right)
Yellow green | Satin stitch | 3 strands

Fern
Forest green | Fern stitch | 2 strands

TIP: If you wish to make a smaller version of this pattern as shown on page 83, feel free to omit the sun. Otherwise, follow the pattern as is, and let the sunlight pour in!

78

STEP 1: Prepare your materials. Following the tutorials in the Getting Started section, transfer the pattern, set your hoop, and separate your floss. Thread your needle with four strands of mustard floss.

STEP 2: Stitch the sun. Using four strands of mustard floss, satin-stitch the sun. Make your first stitch across the widest part of the sun on a diagonal. Fill in one half with compact stitches, then repeat on the other half.

STEP 3: Stitch the sunrays. Using two strands of mustard floss, make a straight stitch for each sunray.

Miniature Greenhouse

STEP 4: Stitch the left philodendron. Using three strands of bright-green floss, outline the stem of the left philodendron with straight stitches. Then, fill in the three leaves with leaf stitch.

STEP 5: Stitch the left agave plant. Using three strands of light-jade floss, fill in the leaves of the left agave plant with vertical satin stitches. To start, make one stitch down the center of a leaf from the tip to the base. Then fill in each side, keeping your stitches small, starting at the edge of the leaf and angling them to meet at the base. Your stitches may overlap slightly.

STEP 6: Stitch the fern. Using two strands of forest-green floss, outline the fern with fern stitch.

STEP 7: Stitch the right agave plant. Using three strands of yellow-green floss, fill in the leaves of the right agave plant with satin stitches, following the same technique as in step 5.

STEP 8: **Stitch the ivy plant.** Using two strands of forest-green floss, outline the ivy plant. Use backstitch for the branches, then add two tiny, parallel straight stitches for each leaf.

STEP 9: **Stitch the pothos plant.** Using two strands of bright-green floss, outline the pothos plant with fern stitch.

STEP 10: **Stitch the greenhouse.** Using two strands of black floss, outline the greenhouse

with backstitches. If you'd like, add in more windowpanes, using perpendicular backstitches or diagonal lines to create a unique look.

STEP 11: **Stitch the cactus.** Using three strands of light-jade floss, fill in the cactus with satin stitches. Start your stitches at the top of each paddle, and stitch down to the base. Each paddle will need only a handful of stitches.

Miniature Greenhouse

STEP 12: **Stitch the right philodendron.** Using three strands of bright-green floss, outline the stems of the philodendron with straight stitches. Then fill in each leaf, using leaf stitch.

STEP 13: **Stitch the philodendron details.** Using two strands of yellow-green floss, make three straight stitches on each philodendron leaf to represent the contrasting leaf veins.

STEP 14: **Finish.** Follow the steps on page 26 to finish the hoop. Remove any transfer pen marks as needed.

Fresh as a Daisy

STITCHES

- Backstitch
- Straight stitch
- French knot

SUPPLIES

- 6" embroidery hoop
- 9" x 9" piece of your chosen fabric
- 1 skein each of white and peach floss
- 1 skein of white tapestry wool or yarn
- Embroidery scissors
- Embroidery needle
- Tapestry needle
- Transfer materials (page 20)
- Finishing materials (page 26)
- Pattern (page 160)

Daisies are one of my favorite flowers, so much so that when we brought home a cream-and-apricot-colored puppy this summer, we gave her the name Daisy! She's proven to be a handful and oh so energetic, but we love her just the same and look forward to many happy years with her in our lives. My embroidery sessions have gotten noticeably shorter since bringing a playful puppy into our family. But a quick and simple project like this one fits in nicely, and I hope it will for you, too!

You'll see the daisies in this design are made with fluffy tapestry wool. This gives the flowers a gentle, ethereal look that I just love. You can sometimes find tapestry wool in the needlepoint aisle at your local craft store, but if not, have no fear. You can substitute regular craft yarn to achieve the same effect. You'll also need a needle with a large eye, known as a tapestry needle. This can also be found in the needlepoint aisle. ▪

TIP: Regular embroidery floss will do just fine if you don't have tapestry wool or yarn on hand. Make a couple of straight stitches to fill in each daisy petal.

Text
White | Backstitch |
6 strands

Daisies
White tapestry wool |
Straight stitch | 1 strand

Daisy Centers
Peach | French knots |
6 strands

Fresh as a Daisy

TIP: Stitch a few of these daisies along the hem of a sweater for a sweet, handmade touch. I added a few daisies to my daughter's blouse (shown on page 89).

STEP 1: Prepare your materials. Following the tutorials in the Getting Started section, transfer your pattern, set your hoop, and separate your floss. Thread your needle with six strands of white floss.

STEP 2: Stitch the text. Using six strands of white floss, outline the letters in backstitch. Keep your stitches short, about ⅛" or shorter, so you can follow the curves of the cursive text.

Fresh as a Daisy

STEP 3: Stitch the daisies. Thread your tapestry needle with a 12" length of white yarn or tapestry wool. Use six straight stitches to make each daisy, with each stitch ending in the center of the flower. Some of the daisies are positioned near the edge of the hoop and require only three petals. As you work, keep the tension on the yarn slightly loose to give your stitches a soft, fluffy effect.

STEP 4: Stitch the daisy centers. Using six strands of peach floss, add a French knot to the center of each daisy. Wrap the floss around your needle two times for each knot.

STEP 5: Finish. Follow the steps on page 26 to finish the hoop. Remove any transfer pen marks as needed.

Meet Me at the Farmers' Market

*I am beginning to learn that it is the sweet,
simple things of life which are the real ones after all.*
LAURA INGALLS WILDER

A Saturday stroll through the local farmers' market is an
absolutely wonderful way to start the day and enjoy some
simple pleasures of life. Supporting local farmers, makers,
and artists; picking out fresh fruits and vegetables; and enjoying
all that the community has to offer make a farmers' market
morning tough to beat! I borrowed some inspiration
from a homegrown and handmade farmers' market
to bring you the patterns in this section.

**Make a list of simple pleasures you are grateful for—
everyday moments that bring you happiness. A perfectly
ripe peach, crafting with a friend, sweater weather,
or an exchange of kindness between strangers.**

Meet Me at the Farmers' Market

STITCHES

- Backstitch
- Straight stitch
- Fern stitch
- Satin stitch
- French knot
- Leaf stitch

SUPPLIES

- 6" embroidery hoop
- 9" x 9" piece of your chosen fabric
- 1 skein each of tan, jade-green, coral, salmon, burnt-orange, yellow, ivory, blue, dark-brown, mustard, and yellow-green floss
- Embroidery scissors
- Embroidery needle
- Transfer materials (page 20)
- Finishing materials (page 26)
- Pattern (page 161)

I had so much fun creating this pattern and filling it with some of the best things you can find at a farmers' market. The fresh produce, flowers, and handmade goods are part of what makes these weekend destinations so wonderful. But we can't forget the rest—getting out into the community, meeting neighbors, filling our refrigerators with nourishing foods, feeling the warm sunshine, hearing live music, and supporting local gardeners, farmers, makers, and artists. These simple pleasures are what nurture our souls and fill up our cups. As you work on this piece, may you be filled with the happiness of a sunny weekend farmers' market! ■

TIP: The guidelines on the pattern for the fruits and veggies will help keep your satin stitches looking neat. Working in small sections like this enables you to see if your stitches are getting off track so you can adjust before it's too late. Remember, it's always okay to pause, remove stitches, and try again if the results are not to your liking.

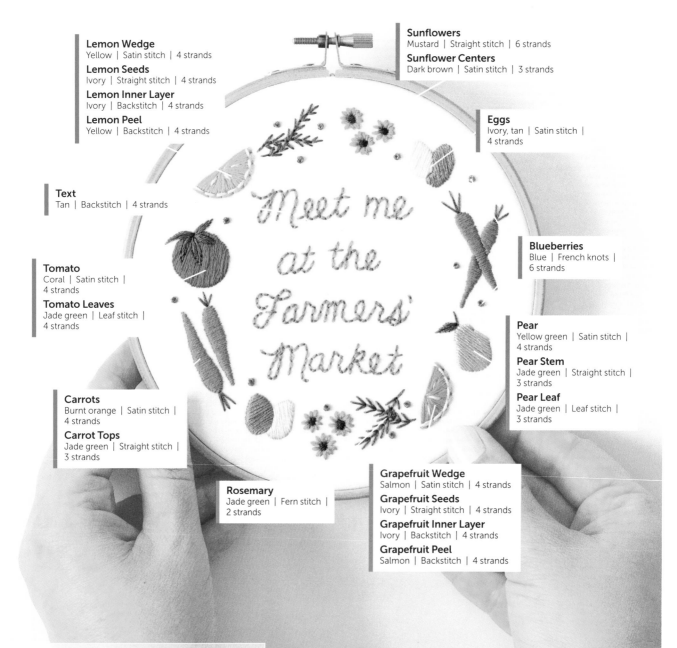

Lemon Wedge
Yellow | Satin stitch | 4 strands
Lemon Seeds
Ivory | Straight stitch | 4 strands
Lemon Inner Layer
Ivory | Backstitch | 4 strands
Lemon Peel
Yellow | Backstitch | 4 strands

Text
Tan | Backstitch | 4 strands

Tomato
Coral | Satin stitch |
4 strands
Tomato Leaves
Jade green | Leaf stitch |
4 strands

Carrots
Burnt orange | Satin stitch |
4 strands
Carrot Tops
Jade green | Straight stitch |
3 strands

Rosemary
Jade green | Fern stitch |
2 strands

Sunflowers
Mustard | Straight stitch | 6 strands
Sunflower Centers
Dark brown | Satin stitch | 3 strands

Eggs
Ivory, tan | Satin stitch |
4 strands

Blueberries
Blue | French knots |
6 strands

Pear
Yellow green | Satin stitch |
4 strands
Pear Stem
Jade green | Straight stitch |
3 strands
Pear Leaf
Jade green | Leaf stitch |
3 strands

Grapefruit Wedge
Salmon | Satin stitch | 4 strands
Grapefruit Seeds
Ivory | Straight stitch | 4 strands
Grapefruit Inner Layer
Ivory | Backstitch | 4 strands
Grapefruit Peel
Salmon | Backstitch | 4 strands

TIP: If you wish, swap out the colors of the fruits and veggies in this design! You can use orange for the citrus fruits, pink for the little French knot berries, or purple and yellow for the carrots. Explore your floss collection and match the colors to your preferences!

STEP 1: Prepare your materials. Following the tutorials in the Getting Started section, transfer your pattern, set your hoop, and separate your floss. Thread your needle with four strands of tan floss.

STEP 2: Stitch the text. Using four strands of tan floss, outline the letters in backstitch.

STEP 3: Stitch the sunflowers. Using six strands of mustard floss, make short straight stitches to create the petals of the sunflowers. Then, using three strands of dark=brown floss, fill the center of each sunflower with satin stitches.

STEP 4: Fill in the eggs. Using four strands of ivory floss, fill in two of the eggs with diagonal satin stitches. Start at the widest part of an egg, filling in one side and then the other. Following the same technique, use four strands of tan floss to fill the remaining two eggs with satin stitch.

Meet Me at the Farmers' Market

STEP 5: Stitch the carrots. Using four strands of burnt-orange floss, fill the carrots with horizontal satin stitches. Then, using three strands of jade-green floss, make three short straight stitches for the carrot tops at the top of each carrot.

STEP 6: Stitch the pear. Using four strands of yellow-green floss, fill in the pear with diagonal satin stitches. Start at the widest part of the pear, filling in one half and then the other. Then, using three strands of jade-green floss, make one straight stitch at the top of the pear for the stem. Using the same floss, fill in the leaf with leaf stitch.

STEP 7: Stitch the grapefruit wedge. Using four strands of salmon floss, fill the grapefruit wedge with satin stitches. Start each stitch at the edge of the wedge and end at the center. Think of your stitches like the spokes of a bicycle wheel and position them accordingly. Using the same floss, backstitch along the outer edge of the wedge to create the peel. Using four strands of ivory floss, add a row of short backstitches between the peel and center of the grapefruit. Using the same floss, add three straight stitches on top of the fruit to create the seeds.

96

STEP 8: Stitch the lemon wedge. Repeat step 7, using four strands of yellow floss to fill in the lemon wedge. Add the details using four strands of ivory floss.

STEP 9: Stitch the rosemary. Using two strands of jade-green floss, outline the rosemary sprigs with fern stitch.

STEP 10: Fill in the tomato. Using four strands of coral floss, fill in the tomato with diagonal satin stitches. Start at the widest part of the tomato,

filling in one half and then the other, leaving the space for the leaves empty. Using four strands of jade-green floss, fill in the leaves with leaf stitch.

STEP 11: Stitch the blueberries. Using six strands of blue floss, make a French knot wherever a dot is shown on the pattern, wrapping the floss around the needle one to two times.

STEP 12: Finish. Follow the steps on page 26 to finish the hoop. Remove any transfer pen marks as needed.

12

Summer Citrus

STITCHES

- Split backstitch
- Leaf stitch
- Lazy daisy
- French knot
- Satin stitch
- Long and short stitch (brick stitch)

SUPPLIES

- 5" embroidery hoop
- 8" x 8" piece of your chosen fabric
- 1 skein each of white, yellow, burnt-orange, salmon, bright-green, and forest-green floss
- Embroidery scissors
- Embroidery needle
- Transfer materials (page 20)
- Finishing materials (page 26)
- Pattern (page 162)

I am often asked about the name of my embroidery art business, Lemon Made Shop. The short and sweet answer is I love lemon everything and thought it was too cute not to use. That's really all there is to it; I love all things lemon and citrus fruits, and I know I'm not alone! Lemon cake, orange cuties, and lime margaritas are well loved by almost everyone. These citrus fruits are rich in vitamins, juicy and refreshing, and a perfect combination of sweet and sour, and add a lively splash of color wherever they're found. After a day of work or play, find yourself a spot in the shade, pour a cold glass of lemonade, and stitch away with me! ■

TIP: Show off your love of citrus fruits by choosing one to stitch on the collar of your shirt or on the corner of a linen napkin.

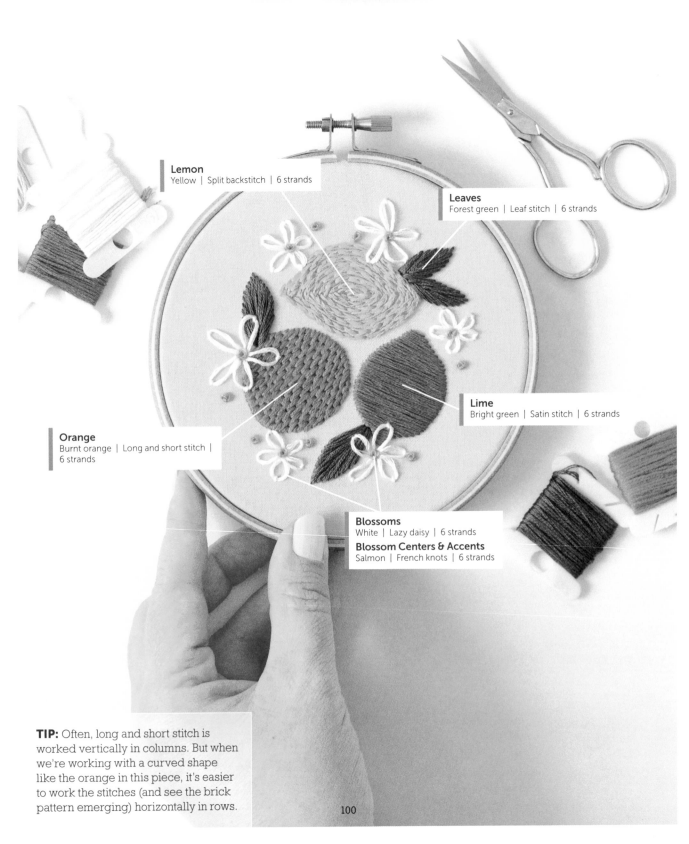

Lemon
Yellow | Split backstitch | 6 strands

Leaves
Forest green | Leaf stitch | 6 strands

Lime
Bright green | Satin stitch | 6 strands

Orange
Burnt orange | Long and short stitch | 6 strands

Blossoms
White | Lazy daisy | 6 strands
Blossom Centers & Accents
Salmon | French knots | 6 strands

TIP: Often, long and short stitch is worked vertically in columns. But when we're working with a curved shape like the orange in this piece, it's easier to work the stitches (and see the brick pattern emerging) horizontally in rows.

STEP 1: Prepare your materials.
Following the tutorials in the Getting Started section, transfer your pattern, set your hoop, and separate your floss. Thread your needle with six strands of yellow floss.

STEP 2: Fill in the lemon. Using six strands of yellow floss, fill in the lemon with split backstitch. Start by stitching along the outline, then add rows working toward the center until the entire shape is filled.

STEP 3: Fill in the lime. Using six strands of bright-green floss, fill in the lime with satin stitches. Start at the widest part and fill in one half and then the other. Remember, when making satin stitches, it can be helpful to divide a shape into smaller sections and fill them in one at a time. This makes it easier to keep your stitches parallel to one another.

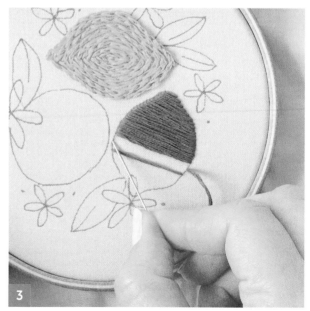

Summer Citrus

STEP 4: Fill in the orange. Using six strands of burnt-orange floss, fill in the orange with long and short stitch. Start with a row of ¼" backstitches across the center of the orange. Add the second row directly below the first one, starting with a ⅛" long stitch followed by ¼" stitches for the rest of the row. Use ¼" stitches for the third row. Start the fourth row with a ⅛" stitch followed by ¼" stitches. Continue adding rows following this pattern until half of the orange is filled in. Repeat to fill in the remaining half.

STEP 5: Fill in the leaves. Using six strands of forest-green floss, fill in each leaf with leaf stitch.

STEP 6: Stitch the flower blossoms. Using six strands of white floss, make five lazy daisy stitches for each flower blossom. Each stitch should end at the center of the blossom.

STEP 7: Stitch the flower centers and accents. Using six strands of salmon floss, make a French knot wherever a dot is shown on the pattern. Wrap the floss around your needle one to two times when making the knots, depending on your desired size.

STEP 8: Finish. Follow the steps on page 26 to finish the hoop. Remove any transfer pen marks as needed.

Cozy Chickens

STITCHES

- Split backstitch
- Backstitch
- Chain stitch
- French knot
- Straight stitch

SUPPLIES

- 6" embroidery hoop
- 9" x 9" piece of your chosen fabric
- 1 skein each of black, ivory, carnation-pink, baby-pink, and burnt-orange floss
- Embroidery scissors
- Embroidery needle
- Transfer materials (page 20)
- Finishing materials (page 26)
- Pattern (page 163)

Growing up, I enjoyed visiting my grandparents' beautiful farm in northern Iowa a few times a year. By that time, my grandparents had retired and didn't have animals living on the farm. Still, my grandma, Marilyn, filled the home with treasured chicken collectibles. My grandma was a hardworking, kind, and quiet woman who loved making things with her hands. Her specialty was woodworking, but she encouraged creativity in any form for her grandkids on the farm. I have so many fond memories of simple summers spent at the farm with my brother and my cousins, and this pattern was made to honor those memories!

You can use some of the embroidery stitches you already know to make these little chicks. Fill in the sweaters with your favorite color scheme and get creative with the sweater patterns. I'll also show you a technique for using fabric appliqué. Appliqué is a tried-and-true method of affixing colorful, patterned fabric to the surface of your embroidery. So, if you have a favorite print or two in your fabric stash, grab a tiny scrap and use it in this project! ◾

TIP: If you want to improvise an intricate pattern for your little chicken, you may want to enlarge the pattern. As it is presented in the book, the sweaters are only about 1 square inch, so there's not a lot of room for elaborate detail. Feel free to enlarge the pattern by using a copier or a craft projector.

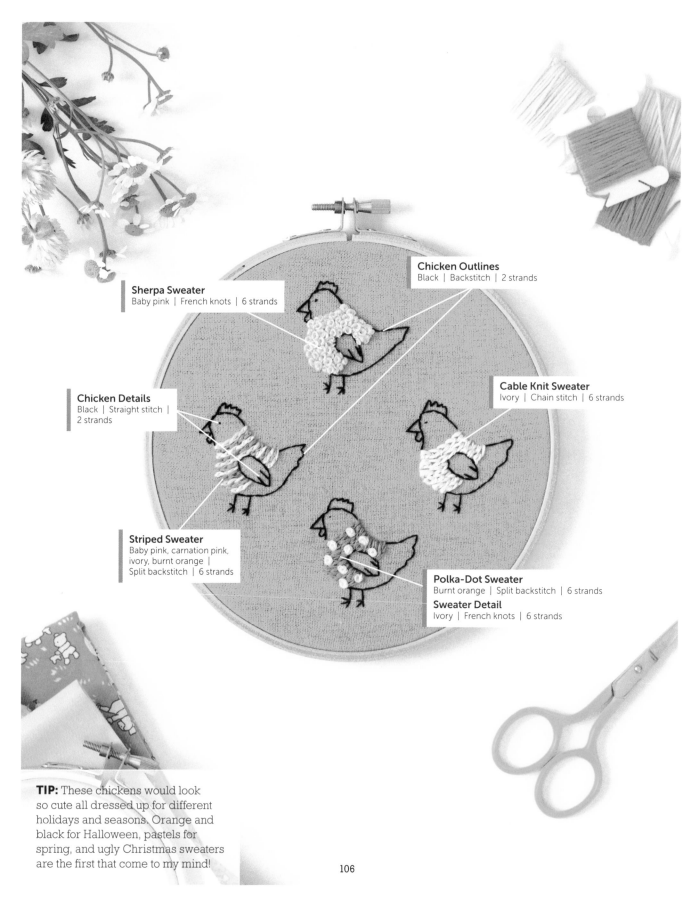

Chicken Outlines
Black | Backstitch | 2 strands

Sherpa Sweater
Baby pink | French knots | 6 strands

Cable Knit Sweater
Ivory | Chain stitch | 6 strands

Chicken Details
Black | Straight stitch |
2 strands

Striped Sweater
Baby pink, carnation pink,
ivory, burnt orange |
Split backstitch | 6 strands

Polka-Dot Sweater
Burnt orange | Split backstitch | 6 strands
Sweater Detail
Ivory | French knots | 6 strands

TIP: These chickens would look
so cute all dressed up for different
holidays and seasons. Orange and
black for Halloween, pastels for
spring, and ugly Christmas sweaters
are the first that come to my mind!

Cozy Chickens

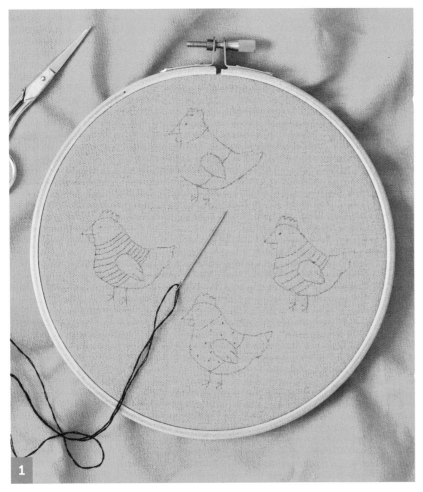

STEP 1: Prepare your materials. Following the tutorials in the Getting Started section, transfer your pattern, set your hoop, and separate your floss. Thread your needle with two strands of black floss.

STEP 2: Stitch the chickens. Using two strands of black floss, outline the four chickens in backstitch. Then, use straight stitches to add the eyes, feet, and wing details.

STEP 3: Fill in the Sherpa sweater. Using six strands of baby-pink floss, fill in the Sherpa sweater with closely spaced French knots.

STEP 4: Fill in the cable knit sweater. Using six strands of ivory floss, fill in the cable knit sweater with rows of chain stitch (see page 144), leaving space for the chicken's wing.

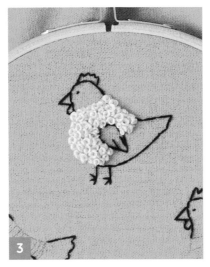

Cozy Chickens

STEP 5: Start filling the polka-dot sweater. Using six strands of burnt orange floss, fill in the polka-dot sweater with rows of split backstitch.

STEP 6: Add French knots. Using six strands of ivory floss, add French knots to the orange sweater to create polka dots. Wrap the floss around your needle two times for each knot.

STEP 7: Fill in the striped sweater. Using six strands of floss, fill in the striped sweater with rows of split backstitches. Use the color pattern baby pink, carnation pink, ivory, and burnt orange. Continue this pattern down the length of the sweater.

STEP 8: Finish. Follow the steps on page 26 to finish the hoop. Remove any transfer pen marks as needed.

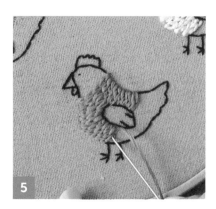

APPLIQUÉ CHICKENS Here is a quick lesson on how to add fabric to your embroidery. This gives you even more options for clothing your cozy chicks in adorable fashions! In addition to the supplies listed at the beginning of this project, you'll also need patterned fabric scraps, sewing pins, and the sweater pattern on page 163. ■

STEP 1: **Prepare your materials.** Following the tutorials in the Getting Started section, transfer your pattern, set your hoop, and separate your floss. Trace and cut out the sweater pattern on page 163 to use as a template. Thread your needle with two strands of black floss.

STEP 2: **Cut out the sweater.** Using a transfer pen, trace the sweater pattern onto the right side of a small scrap of patterned fabric, then cut it out.

STEP 3: **Pin the sweater.** Using sewing pins, attach the sweater to the hooped fabric, positioning it on top of the chicken.

STEP 4: **Attach the sweater.** Using two strands of black floss, stitch around the edge of the sweater, using straight or running stitches to secure it to the hooped fabric. Alternatively, you could use French knots placed in a polka-dot pattern to attach the sweater.

STEP 5: **Stitch the chicken.** Using two strands of black floss, outline the chicken in backstitch. Use straight stitches to add the details, including the wing, legs, and eye.

STEP 6: **Finish.** Follow the steps on page 26 to finish the hoop. Remove any transfer pen marks as needed.

Good Things Take Time

STITCHES

- Split backstitch
- Backstitch
- Straight stitch
- French knot
- Satin stitch
- Fern stitch

SUPPLIES

- 5" embroidery hoop
- 8" x 8" piece of your chosen fabric
- 1 skein each of tan, bright-green, salmon, ivory, white, lavender, baby-pink, burnt-orange, pink, yellow, and light-jade floss
- Pink and light-brown colored pencils
- Embroidery scissors
- Embroidery needle
- Transfer materials (page 20)
- Finishing materials (page 26)
- Pattern (page 164)

Even though we are accustomed to having all that we need immediately at our fingertips, we know flowers take a season to bloom. A skill can take months to learn. A relationship can take years to mature. A goal is not reached overnight. Patience and perseverance allow us to see things through, especially over a long period. For me personally, waiting is not one of my strengths, but I really believe that good things take time, which is true with embroidery! Let this be your mantra today. Spend a few quiet hours on this project, step away from the hustle and bustle of life, and enjoy every minute of it.

This project, inspired by a small flower farm stand at my farmers' market, is another one that uses colored pencils. If you don't have any colored pencils on hand, simply keep your fabric as is. You can still add color to the flower stand awning if you like by filling it with alternating bands with satin stitch. ■

TIP: Sometimes, the pattern lines can become warped when you stretch your fabric on the hoop. Let the weave of the fabric guide you in creating right angles and clean lines as you stretch the fabric. Be sure to use a transfer pen that can be erased. Then, when you remove your transfer pen marks, you'll have nice clean stitch lines, even if the pattern transfer wasn't perfect.

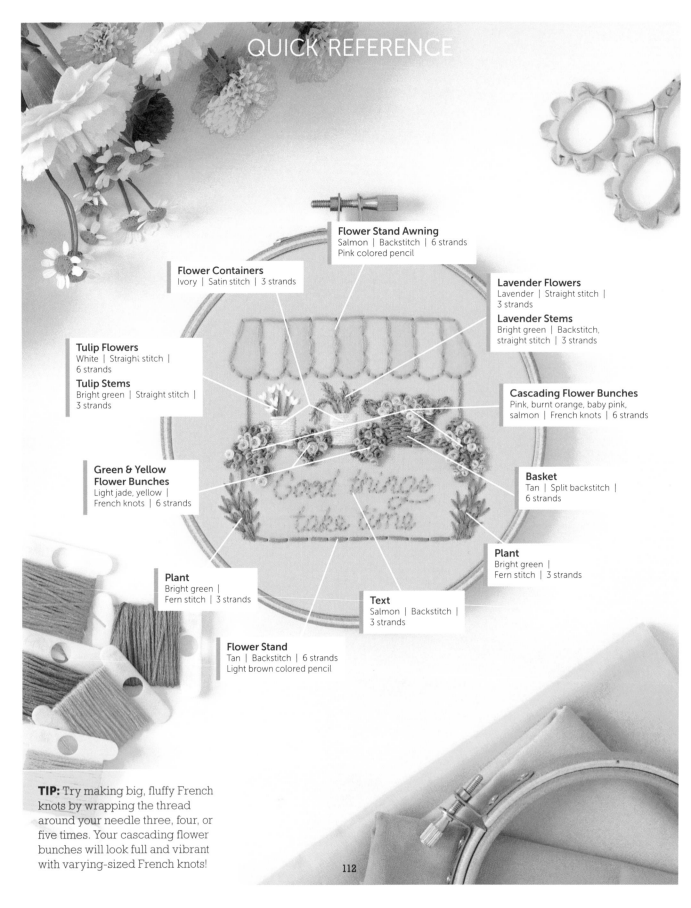

Flower Stand Awning
Salmon | Backstitch | 6 strands
Pink colored pencil

Flower Containers
Ivory | Satin stitch | 3 strands

Lavender Flowers
Lavender | Straight stitch |
3 strands

Lavender Stems
Bright green | Backstitch,
straight stitch | 3 strands

Tulip Flowers
White | Straight stitch |
6 strands

Tulip Stems
Bright green | Straight stitch |
3 strands

Cascading Flower Bunches
Pink, burnt orange, baby pink,
salmon | French knots | 6 strands

**Green & Yellow
Flower Bunches**
Light jade, yellow |
French knots | 6 strands

Basket
Tan | Split backstitch |
6 strands

Plant
Bright green |
Fern stitch | 3 strands

Plant
Bright green |
Fern stitch | 3 strands

Text
Salmon | Backstitch |
3 strands

Flower Stand
Tan | Backstitch | 6 strands
Light brown colored pencil

TIP: Try making big, fluffy French knots by wrapping the thread around your needle three, four, or five times. Your cascading flower bunches will look full and vibrant with varying-sized French knots!

112

STEP 1: Prepare your materials. Following the tutorials in the Getting Started section, transfer your pattern, set your hoop, and separate your floss. Thread your needle with six strands of tan floss.

STEP 2: Color the awning. Using a pink colored pencil, color in every other band of the flower stand awning. Use even, gentle strokes to apply the color.

STEP 3: Color the flower stand. Using a light-brown colored pencil, color in the base of the flower stand.

STEP 4: Stitch the flower stand. Using six strands of tan floss, outline the flower stand in backstitch.

Good Things Take Time

STEP 5: Stitch the flower stand awning. Using six strands of salmon floss, outline the flower stand awning in backstitch.

STEP 6: Stitch the text. Using three strands of salmon floss, outline the letters in backstitch. Keep the stitches short and even so you can follow the curves of the text. If the colored pencil you used to color the flower stand is dark, you may want to use a floss color other than salmon to provide more contrast.

STEP 7: Stitch the bottom plants. Using three strands of bright-green floss, outline the plants at the bottom of the flower stand with fern stitch. Your stitches will lie right over the tan floss from step 4.

STEP 8: Fill in the flower canisters. Using three strands of ivory floss, fill in the flower canisters with horizontal satin stitches.

STEP 9: Stitch the flower stems. Using three strands of bright-green floss, outline the stems of the flowers in the canisters. Use straight stitches for the straight stems and backstitches for the curved stems.

STEP 10: Stitch the tulips. Using six strands of white floss, stitch the tulips by making two short straight stitches that share an end point at the top of each stem in the left canister.

STEP 11: Stitch the lavender flowers. Using three strands of lavender floss, add the lavender flowers to the stems in the right canister. Start by making a straight stitch at the top of the stem. Then work your way down the stem, alternating stitches on either side.

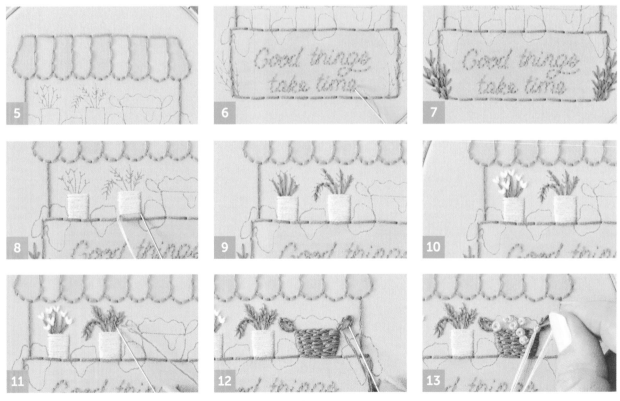

STEP 12: Fill in the basket. Using six strands of tan floss, fill in the basket with horizontal rows of split backstitch. Then, use split backstitch to create the handles.

STEP 13: Start filling the pink flower bunches. Using six strands of baby-pink floss, add French knots to the basket and each side of the flower stand, leaving space for additional colors in the following steps. Wrap the floss around your needle one to three times to create varying sizes of French knots. Allow the flowers to spill out of the basket, stitching right on top of the tan stitches. For the flower bunches on the sides of the flower stand, stitch over the tan floss outline.

STEP 14: Finish filling the pink flower bunches. Continue adding French knots to the flower bunches using six strands of salmon, pink, and burnt-orange floss.

STEP 15: Fill in the remaining flower bunches. Add French knots to the flower bunches in the center of the flower stand, using six strands of light-jade and yellow floss. Wrap the floss around your needle one to three times to vary the sides of the knots.

STEP 16: Finish. Follow the steps on page 26 to finish the hoop. Remove any transfer pen marks as needed.

14

15

16

MY HAPPY PLACE

Take a Hike

Climb the mountains and get their good tidings. Nature's peace will flow into you as sunshine flows into trees. The winds will blow their own freshness into you, and the storms their energy, while cares will drop away from you like the leaves of Autumn.

JOHN MUIR

A hike is a fresh-air-filled activity anyone can love. Maybe you're looking for a dynamic way to exercise or a peaceful and serene walk with your dog. Maybe you need some solitude, or you're looking for a group activity with your family and friends. Do you like a quick-paced hike to challenge yourself or a slow leisurely pace to get up close and observe nature's treasures? (The second is definitely more my jam!) Either way, as you experience the delight of crisp, fragrant air; lush green trees; or beautiful scenery, just remember to take good care of our earth while it takes good care of you. Take a look at some of these hiking-inspired projects and see what you can embroider today!

**Grab a journal and write about a time
you felt at peace or energized by being in nature.**

Leaf Guide

STITCHES

- Backstitch
- Straight stitch

SUPPLIES

- 6" embroidery hoop
- 9" x 9" piece of your chosen fabric
- 1 skein of white floss
- Embroidery scissors
- Embroidery needle
- Transfer materials (page 20)
- Finishing materials (page 26)
- Pattern (page 165)

I've always been enamored with trees and their intricate leaf shapes and patterns. One of my favorite memories from high school is taking nature walks during biology class, learning how to identify trees on the basis of their leaves. We used a little tree identification book, and I still keep it on my bookshelf today, which may make me a little nerdy. I also think fondly of the gorgeous redwoods of California, the brightly colored maples of my hometown in central Illinois in the fall, and the majestic oaks of Texas. I created this embroidery project as an ode to trees, the beautiful, gentle giants that make our world so wonderful.

You'll find that this project is an easy one to stitch, using backstitch and straight stitch only. Embroider the design on a tote bag or keep it in the hoop to be displayed all year-round or just when autumn comes. ■

TIP: Try stitching a leaf or two on a shirt pocket or collar, then fill each with a satin stitch.

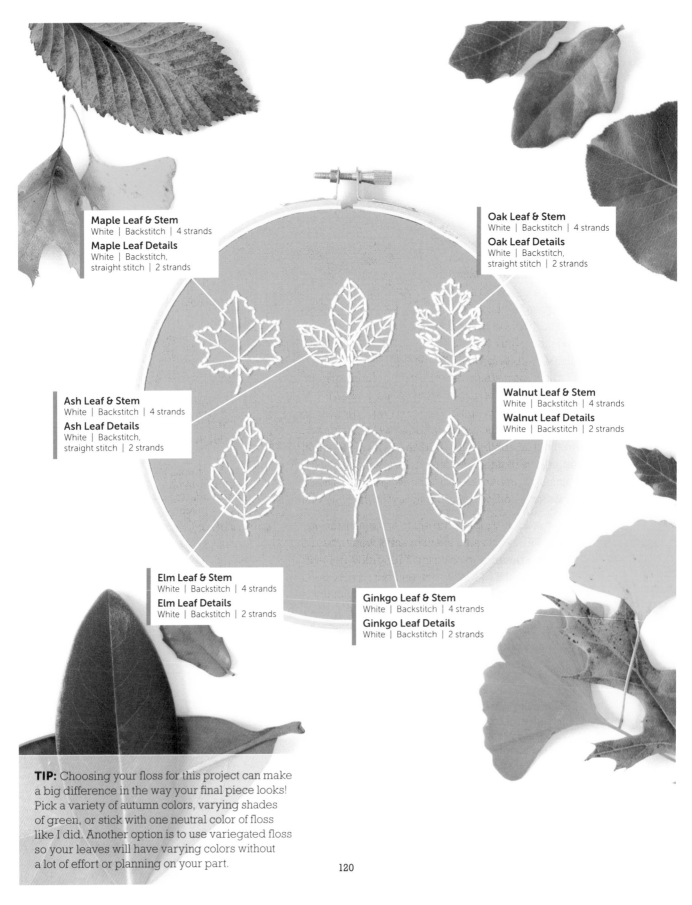

Maple Leaf & Stem
White | Backstitch | 4 strands
Maple Leaf Details
White | Backstitch,
straight stitch | 2 strands

Oak Leaf & Stem
White | Backstitch | 4 strands
Oak Leaf Details
White | Backstitch,
straight stitch | 2 strands

Ash Leaf & Stem
White | Backstitch | 4 strands
Ash Leaf Details
White | Backstitch,
straight stitch | 2 strands

Walnut Leaf & Stem
White | Backstitch | 4 strands
Walnut Leaf Details
White | Backstitch | 2 strands

Elm Leaf & Stem
White | Backstitch | 4 strands
Elm Leaf Details
White | Backstitch | 2 strands

Ginkgo Leaf & Stem
White | Backstitch | 4 strands
Ginkgo Leaf Details
White | Backstitch | 2 strands

TIP: Choosing your floss for this project can make a big difference in the way your final piece looks! Pick a variety of autumn colors, varying shades of green, or stick with one neutral color of floss like I did. Another option is to use variegated floss so your leaves will have varying colors without a lot of effort or planning on your part.

120

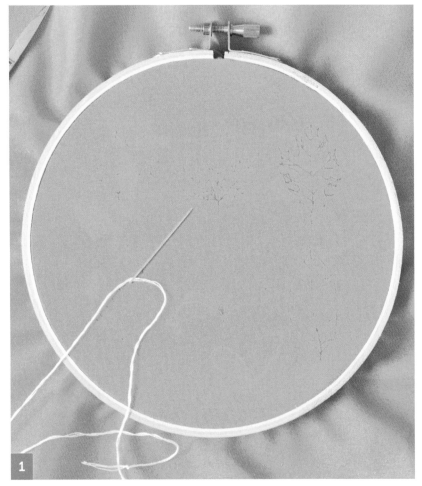

STEP 1: Prepare your materials. Following the tutorials in the Getting Started section, transfer your pattern, set your hoop, and separate your floss. Thread your needle with four strands of white floss.

STEP 2: Stitch the maple leaf. Using four strands of white floss, outline the maple leaf and stem in backstitch. As you work on this piece, keep your stitches very short to make it easier to follow the curves of the leaves.

STEP 3: Add the maple leaf details. Using two strands of white floss, create the leaf veins. Use backstitches for the main veins and straight stitches for the smaller veins.

STEP 4: Stitch the ash leaves. Using four strands of white floss, outline the ash leaves and stem with backstitch.

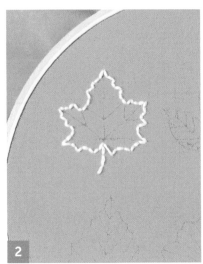

Leaf Guide

STEP 5: Add the ash leaf details. Using two strands of white floss, create the leaf veins. Use backstitches for the main veins and straight stitches for the smaller veins.

STEP 6: Stitch the oak leaf. Using four strands of white floss, outline the oak leaf and stem in backstitch.

STEP 7: Add the oak leaf details. Using two strands of white floss, create the leaf veins. Use backstitches for the main veins and straight stitches for the smaller veins.

STEP 8: Stitch the elm leaf. Using four strands of white floss, outline the elm leaf and stem in backstitch.

STEP 9: Add the elm leaf details. Using two strands of white floss, backstitch the leaf veins of the elm leaf.

STEP 10: Stitch the ginkgo leaf. Using four strands of white floss, outline the ginkgo leaf and stem in backstitch.

STEP 11: Add the ginkgo leaf details. Using two strands of white floss, backstitch the leaf veins of the ginkgo leaf. Make the stitches short so it's easier to follow the curved lines.

STEP 12: Stitch the walnut leaf. Using four strands of white floss, outline the walnut leaf and stem in backstitch.

STEP 13: Add the walnut leaf details. Using two strands of white floss, backstitch the leaf veins of the walnut leaf.

STEP 14: Finish. Follow the steps on page 26 to finish the hoop. Remove any transfer pen marks as needed.

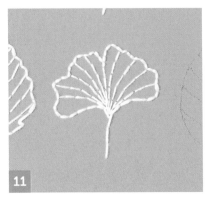

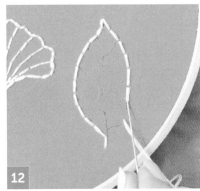

Woodland Wonders

STITCHES

- Split backstitch
- Satin stitch
- Straight stitch
- French knot
- Lazy daisy
- Backstitch

SUPPLIES

- 4" embroidery hoop
- 7" x 7" piece of your chosen fabric
- 1 skein each of coral, ivory, yellow, yellow-green, olive-green, and jade-green floss
- Gold seed beads (optional)
- Beading needle (optional)
- Embroidery scissors
- Embroidery needle
- Transfer materials (page 20)
- Finishing materials (page 26)
- Pattern (page 159)

When was the last time you stopped and examined the tiny wonders of our earth? A seashell on the beach, an acorn on the sidewalk, the fuzzy yellow pollen on a flower, or a dewy blade of grass? Whenever you spot something in nature that catches your attention, lean in with childlike wonder and consider it a gift. But before you go and do that, focus your attention on creating this adorable toadstool mushroom resting in a mossy woodland, and soak in the wonder of it all!

For this project, we'll incorporate some tiny gold seed beads. You can find these in the beading aisle of any craft store. You'll also need a very thin beading needle that can pass through the beads. If you don't have beads on hand, you can substitute French knots. You'll notice that I chose felt as my background fabric, and I encourage you to try it as well! Wool felt is readily available in a myriad of colors and gives you a welcome change of texture from traditional embroidery fabrics like cotton or linen. However, you can, of course, use whatever fabric inspires you! ■

TIP: If you use a dark or thick fabric (like felt), use carbon transfer paper to transfer the pattern onto the fabric.

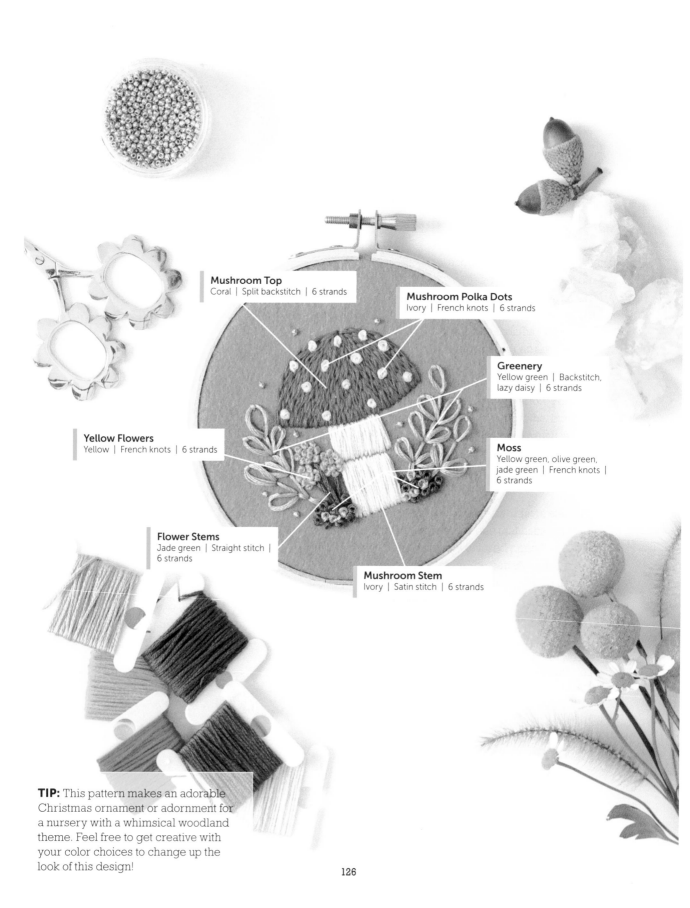

Mushroom Top
Coral | Split backstitch | 6 strands

Mushroom Polka Dots
Ivory | French knots | 6 strands

Greenery
Yellow green | Backstitch, lazy daisy | 6 strands

Yellow Flowers
Yellow | French knots | 6 strands

Moss
Yellow green, olive green, jade green | French knots | 6 strands

Flower Stems
Jade green | Straight stitch | 6 strands

Mushroom Stem
Ivory | Satin stitch | 6 strands

TIP: This pattern makes an adorable Christmas ornament or adornment for a nursery with a whimsical woodland theme. Feel free to get creative with your color choices to change up the look of this design!

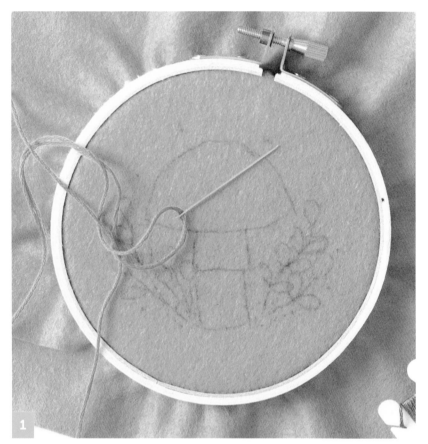

STEP 1: Prepare your materials. Following the tutorials in the Getting Started section, transfer your pattern, set your hoop, and separate your floss. Thread your needle with six strands of coral floss.

STEP 2: Fill in the mushroom top. Using six strands of coral floss, fill in the mushroom top with rows of split backstitch. Divide the mushroom top into sections similar to an umbrella to guide your stitches.

STEP 3: Fill in the mushroom stem. Using six strands of ivory floss, fill in both sections of the mushroom stem with vertical satin stitches.

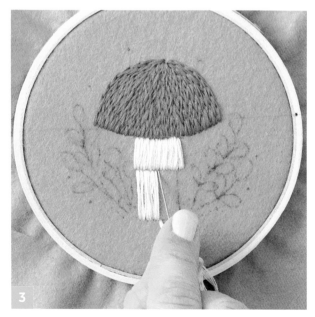

Woodland Wonders

STEP 4: Add the mushroom dots. Using six strands of ivory floss, add French knots to create the dots on the mushroom top. To make the dots stand out, wrap the floss around your needle three to four times.

STEP 5: Stitch the greenery. Using six strands of yellow-green floss, outline the stems of the greenery in backstitch. Then, use lazy daisy stitches to create the leaves.

STEP 6: Stitch the flower stems. Using six strands of jade-green floss, outline the flower stems with straight stitches.

STEP 7: Fill in the yellow flowers. Using six strands of yellow floss, fill in each flower with a cluster of compact, closely spaced French knots, wrapping the floss around your needle one to two times.

STEP 8: Stitch the moss. Using six strands of jade-green floss, add a few French knots around the mushroom base. Repeat with the yellow-green and olive-green floss until the areas are filled with closely spaced French knots, creating the effect of a mossy forest floor.

STEP 9: Add the beads. Thread the beading needle with one strand of yellow floss, knotting the tail several times. Bring the needle and floss to the front of the fabric where you want to add a bead. Pick up a bead with the needle and string it along the floss down to the fabric. Finish the stitch by pushing the needle through the fabric next to the bead. Run the needle and floss through the bead once or twice more to secure it. Add a bead to each dot shown on the pattern. If you don't want to add beads, you can use six strands of yellow floss to make French knots instead.

STEP 10: Finish. Follow the steps on page 26 to finish the hoop. Remove any transfer pen marks as needed.

10

Brilliant Butterfly

STITCHES

- Backstitch
- Straight stitch
- Satin stitch
- Fern stitch
- Pistil stitch

SUPPLIES

- 5" embroidery hoop
- 8" x 8" piece of your chosen fabric
- 1 skein each of mustard, burnt-orange, black, ivory, yellow-green, bright-green, salmon, coral, and metallic gold floss
- Embroidery scissors
- Embroidery needle
- Transfer materials (page 20)
- Finishing materials (page 26)
- Pattern (page 166)

This past spring, my kids and I planted cosmos, zinnias, poppies, and daisies from seed in a little flower bed in our backyard. We watched them grow from tiny sprouts (eaten mainly by uninvited rabbits) to towering stems, which finally exploded with brilliant pinks and oranges in midsummer. We had the joy and excitement of viewing many different hummingbirds, bees, and butterflies up close. The kids and I identified giant swallowtails, monarchs, painted ladies, and others. Each visit by one of these lovely creatures was a little bit of magic and made all the effort of growing the garden worthwhile. I cannot wait for next summer to see what we can do!

I made this design in honor of all of those pretty (and pretty important) pollinators who graced us with their presence this summer. You'll see gold metallic floss, sold with the embroidery floss in your local craft store, used in some of the elements. If it's not available for you, try using two strands of a warm, golden-colored cotton floss instead. Either way, come along and stitch this bright and brilliant butterfly with me. ■

TIP: Metallic floss can be found in most craft stores with regular embroidery floss. It comes on a spool or in a standard skein, and the strands don't need to be divided. You'll want to work with lengths of 12" or less to avoid pesky tangles because this stiff and inflexible floss tends to be more challenging to untangle than regular floss. Give it a try and see what you think!

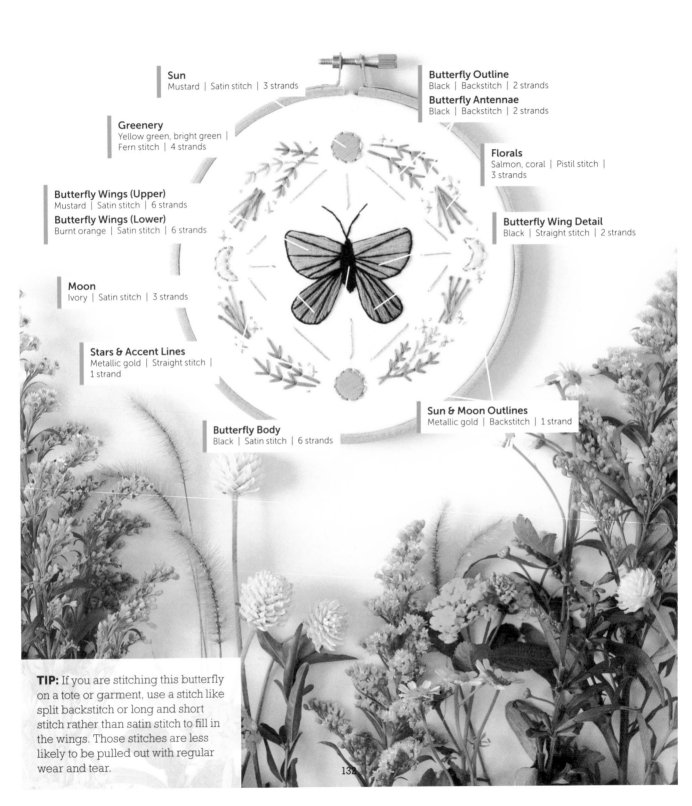

Sun
Mustard | Satin stitch | 3 strands

Greenery
Yellow green, bright green |
Fern stitch | 4 strands

Butterfly Wings (Upper)
Mustard | Satin stitch | 6 strands

Butterfly Wings (Lower)
Burnt orange | Satin stitch | 6 strands

Moon
Ivory | Satin stitch | 3 strands

Stars & Accent Lines
Metallic gold | Straight stitch |
1 strand

Butterfly Body
Black | Satin stitch | 6 strands

Butterfly Outline
Black | Backstitch | 2 strands

Butterfly Antennae
Black | Backstitch | 2 strands

Florals
Salmon, coral | Pistil stitch |
3 strands

Butterfly Wing Detail
Black | Straight stitch | 2 strands

Sun & Moon Outlines
Metallic gold | Backstitch | 1 strand

TIP: If you are stitching this butterfly on a tote or garment, use a stitch like split backstitch or long and short stitch rather than satin stitch to fill in the wings. Those stitches are less likely to be pulled out with regular wear and tear.

STEP 1: Prepare your materials. Following the tutorials in the Getting Started section, transfer your pattern, set your hoop, and separate your floss. Thread your needle with six strands of mustard floss.

STEP 2: Fill in the upper wings. Using six strands of mustard floss, fill in the top two wings of the butterfly with horizontal satin stitches. Start each stitch at the outer edge of the wing and end at the butterfly's body. Some of your stitches will need to overlap to fit the narrow part of the wings closest to the body.

STEP 3: Fill in the lower wings. Using six strands of burnt-orange floss, fill in the bottom two wings of the butterfly with satin stitches. Again, start your stitches at the edge of the wing and end at the body, overlapping stitches as needed to fit the narrow area.

STEP 4: Fill in the body. Using six strands of black floss, fill in the butterfly's body with a few vertical satin stitches.

Brilliant Butterfly

STEP 5: Stitch the antennae. Using two strands of black floss, backstitch the butterfly's antennae.

STEP 6: Stitch the outline and wing details. Using two strands of black floss, backstitch the outline of the butterfly. Then add straight stitches over top of the orange and yellow floss of the wings to create the detail lines.

STEP 7: Stitch the greenery. Using four strands of yellow-green floss, outline several pieces of the greenery with fern stitch. Then, use four strands of bright-green floss to outline the remaining pieces of greenery with fern stitch.

STEP 8: Stitch the florals. Using three strands of salmon floss, add three pistil stitches to each of the four floral bunches. Then, use three strands of coral floss to fill in the remaining stitches in the floral bunches. See page 146 for a detailed description of the pistil stitch.

STEP 9: Fill in the suns. Using three strands of mustard floss, fill in the two suns with satin stitch.

STEP 10: Fill in the moons. Using three strands of ivory floss, fill in the two moons with satin stitch.

STEP 11: Outline the suns and moons. Using one strand of metallic gold floss, outline the suns and moons with short backstitches. Metallic floss does not need to be split. Work with short lengths to keep the floss from fraying and avoid tangles. Alternatively, use two strands of any cotton floss to outline the shapes.

STEP 12: Stitch the gold accent lines. Using one strand of metallic gold floss, add a straight stitch for each accent line in the center of the pattern.

STEP 13: Stitch the stars and sparkles. Using one strand of metallic gold floss, add the stars and sparkles with straight stitches. The stars are made with two short perpendicular stitches. The small sparkles are made with one tiny straight stitch.

STEP 14: Finish. Follow the steps on page 26 to finish the hoop. Remove any transfer pen marks as needed.

My Happy Place

STITCHES

- Split backstitch
- Backstitch
- Straight stitch
- French knot
- Satin stitch

SUPPLIES

- 5" embroidery hoop
- 8" x 8" piece of your chosen fabric
- 1 skein each of gray, mustard, light-apricot, blue, dark-brown, and forest-green loss
- Embroidery scissors
- Embroidery needle
- Transfer materials (page 20)
- Finishing materials (page 26)
- Pattern (page 167)

I want to transport you to a happy place with our final project! Think of your favorite spot in nature, a national or state park, or a preserve with a beautiful view. Imagine the crisp air, fragrant scent of evergreen pines, cool flowing water, and warm sunshine. Do you feel peaceful and serene here? Or refreshed, or energized?

For many of us, a walk or hike through a forest trail can make us feel grounded and even humbled to be surrounded by towering evergreens and mountains and to think of all the years they have been here before us. I hope this final embroidery project brings some of those feelings and memories to you today and anytime you take a look at your finished piece. Find your happy place, whether it's your cozy home, a favorite park, or a coffee shop, and settle in to stitch! ∎

TIP: Create the fluffy clouds by making very full French knots. Experiment with wrapping the floss around your needle two to five times or more. Try altering the tension of the floss to make the knots loose. You can also use your needle to gently pull at a finished knot to make it more fluffy.

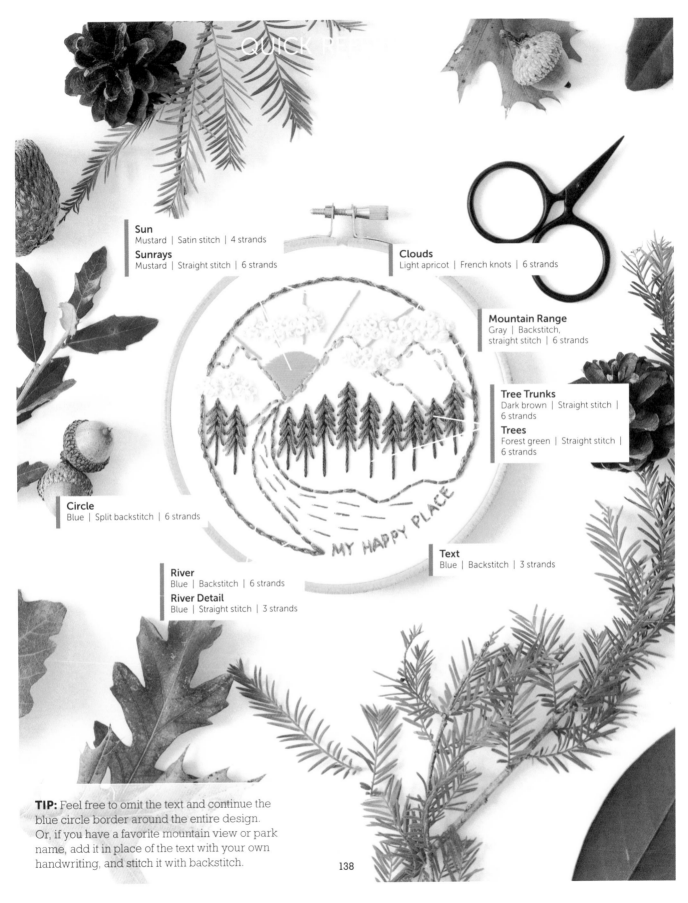

Sun
Mustard | Satin stitch | 4 strands
Sunrays
Mustard | Straight stitch | 6 strands

Clouds
Light apricot | French knots | 6 strands

Mountain Range
Gray | Backstitch,
straight stitch | 6 strands

Tree Trunks
Dark brown | Straight stitch |
6 strands
Trees
Forest green | Straight stitch |
6 strands

Circle
Blue | Split backstitch | 6 strands

Text
Blue | Backstitch | 3 strands

River
Blue | Backstitch | 6 strands
River Detail
Blue | Straight stitch | 3 strands

MY HAPPY PLACE

TIP: Feel free to omit the text and continue the blue circle border around the entire design. Or, if you have a favorite mountain view or park name, add it in place of the text with your own handwriting, and stitch it with backstitch.

138

STEP 1: Prepare your materials. Following the tutorials in the Getting Started section, transfer your pattern, set your hoop, and separate your floss. Thread your needle with six strands of gray floss.

STEP 2: Stitch the mountain range. Using six strands of gray floss, outline the mountain range in backstitch. Use short straight stitches to add a few details. If you wish, you can use white floss for the small detail lines to create a snowy effect.

STEP 3: Fill in the sun. Using four strands of mustard floss, fill in the sun with horizontal satin stitches.

STEP 4: Stitch the sunrays. Using six strands of mustard floss, create the sunrays with long straight stitches.

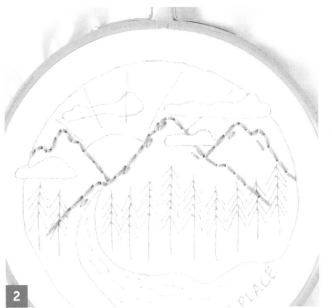

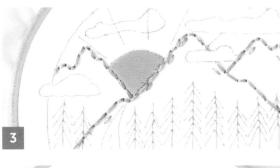

My Happy Place

STEP 5: Fill in the clouds. Using six strands of light-apricot floss, fill in the clouds with closely spaced, fluffy French knots. Wrap the floss around your needle two to five times to make knots of varying sizes. Hold the floss loosely to make the knots large and fluffy.

STEP 6: Stitch the border. Using six strands of blue floss, add the circular border around the design with split backstitch.

STEP 7: Stitch the river. Using six strands of blue floss, outline the river in backstitch.

STEP 8: Stitch the tree trunks. Using six strands of dark-brown floss, add a long straight stitch for each tree trunk. Begin each stitch at the tree's base and end it about ⅛" from the top, leaving that last bit to be stitched in the next step.

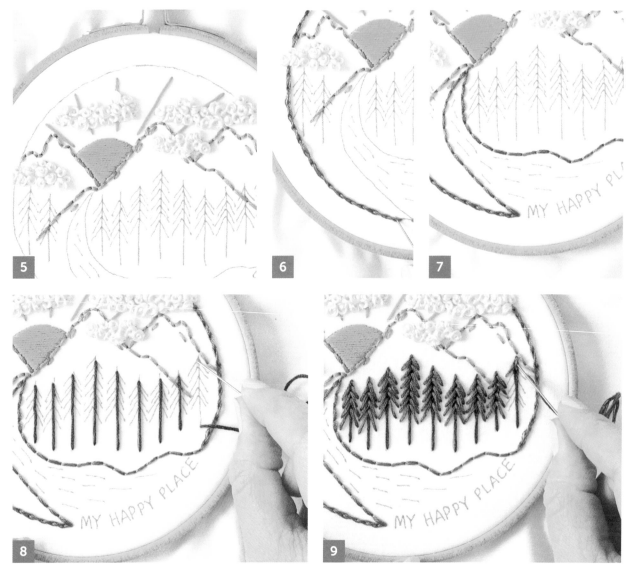

STEP 9: Stitch the tree branches. Using six strands of forest-green floss, make the evergreen branches with straight stitches. Start with a ¼" long straight stitch at the top of each tree, ending in the dark-brown floss of the trunk. Then, add straight stitches down each side of the trunk. Start each stitch at the end of the branch and finish it at the trunk.

STEP 10: Stitch the river details. Using three strands of blue floss, add the river details with straight stitches.

STEP 11: Stitch the text. Using three strands of blue floss, outline the letters in backstitch. Use short, uniform stitches to follow the curves of the letters.

STEP 12: Finish. Follow the steps on page 26 to finish the hoop. Remove any transfer pen marks as needed.

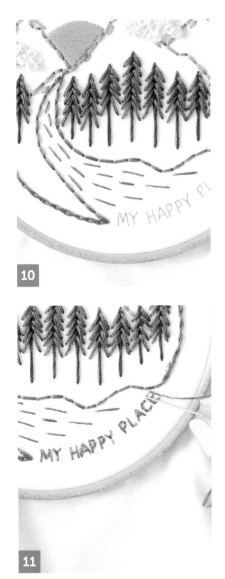

Appendix

This is your go-to reference for detailed instructions and diagrams about making the stitches in this book. Use the stitch library whenever you need a little guidance to remind yourself how to make a specific stitch. You'll also find the patterns for each project here, and a floss color index with the DMC floss color numbers I used.

Appendix

Embroidery Stitch Library

Backstitch. This stitch is used for outlining. Make a straight stitch about ¼" long. Bring the needle up through the fabric about ¼" from the end of the first stitch. Stitch backward, pushing your needle through the hole at the end of the first stitch. Your stitches will be touching and sharing the same hole in the fabric.

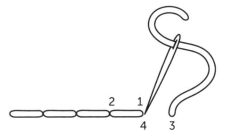

Chain Stitch. Start with a very short straight stitch, but do not pull the thread all the way through. Instead, use your fingers to hold it in a loop above the fabric. Bring your needle up ¼" away from the first stitch and feed it through the loop. Pull the thread tight to bring the loop down against the fabric, but not so tight that the loop loses its shape. Return your needle to the back of the fabric through the same hole it came out of (it will be in the center of the loop). Don't pull it tight, but form another loop. Bring your needle up ¼" from the stitch, feed it through the loop, and pull the loop tight. Return the needle through the same hole it came out of, forming a new loop. Repeat.

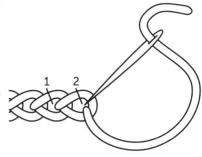

Fern Stitch. Use this stitch to outline plants, feathers, or other botanical designs. Start by making a row of backstitches for the center line—this could be straight or curved. Then add short straight stitches where the backstitches meet. Experiment with making the straight stitches the same length or varying lengths.

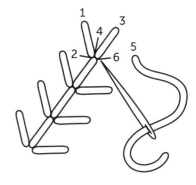

French Knot. Bring your needle up through the fabric. With one hand, hold the floss perpendicular to the fabric, gripping it tightly a few inches above the fabric. With your other hand, place your needle against the back of the floss and hold it in place while you wrap the floss around it one or two times (the more wraps, the larger the finished knot). With the looped floss on it, return your needle through the fabric, just next to the starting point. Use one hand to hold the floss out to the side, keeping it taut. As you pull the needle through the fabric, gradually and steadily release the floss. You'll be left with a tidy knot on the surface of the fabric.

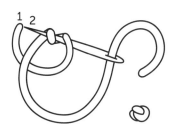

Lazy Daisy Stitch (Detached Chain Stitch). Lazy daisy stitches can be used the make petals or leaves. Start with a very tiny stitch, but do not pull the thread all the way through. Instead, let it form a loop on top of the fabric and gently hold it in place. Bring your needle up through the fabric where you want the top of the loop to be, and feed it through the loop. Pull the thread tight to bring the loop down against the fabric. Enter the fabric just above where the needle came out, capturing the top of the loop in the stitch.

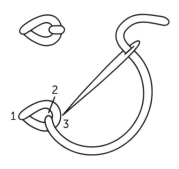

Leaf Stitch. This stitch is perfect for filling in leaves. Start with one straight stitch down the center of the leaf from the tip to about three-quarters of the way to the base. Start the second stitch by bringing the needle out on the top left side of the first stitch at the edge of the leaf. Cross over the first stitch, ending just to the right of it in the middle of the leaf. Repeat on the opposite side of the leaf. Continue stitching to the base of the leaf, keeping your stitches parallel to one another on each side.

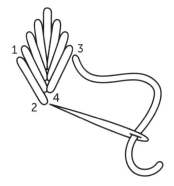

Embroidery Stitch Library, *continued*

Long and Short Stitch (Brick Stitch). Work in horizontal rows. For the first row, alternate ¼" and ⅛" straight stitches. For the following rows, use ¼" stitches. Because of the way you stitched the first row, the stitches in the subsequent rows will have alternating end points. This is a useful fill stitch.

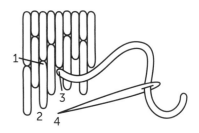

Padded Satin Stitch. This is a fill stitch used to add a little extra dimension to your embroidery. Begin by filling in a shape with a base layer of seed stitch, satin stitch, or long and short stitch. It doesn't matter what this layer looks like, because it will be covered up in the next step. Add a layer of uniform, compact sating stitches over top of the base layer. To create even more dimension, add multiple base layers.

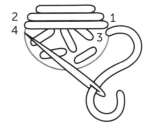

Pistil Stitch. Pistil stitch is a variation of the French knot and is useful in making flower details. Follow the same steps for making a French knot, bringing your needle up through the fabric and wrapping the floss around it. Instead of ending the stitch right next to the starting point, make a longer stitch about ¼" in length to finish.

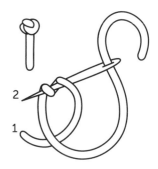

Satin Stitch. Satin stitch allows you to fill a space with smooth, flat stitches. It's especially useful for filling small shapes. Start the stitch on one side of the shape you're filling, and end it directly opposite on the other side of the shape. Repeat, making close, parallel stitches that fill the shape from one end to the other.

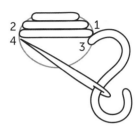

Seed Stitch. This is a fill stitch made of a group of straight stitches. The stitches are even in length but placed randomly. They can be spread out, packed in closely, and even overlapping. You can use one or more floss colors.

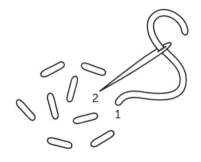

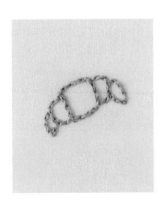

Split Backstitch. This stitch is just like backstitch, but instead of ending in the same hole as the previous stitch, you'll end in the middle of the first stitch, splitting the floss. Make a straight stitch about ¼" long. Bring the needle up through the fabric about ¼" from the end of the first stitch. Stitch backward, pushing your needle through the middle of the first stitch, splitting the floss strands in half. Because of the split, this stitch works best with either four or six strands of floss. Use this stitch for a textured outline.

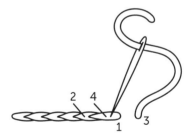

Embroidery Stitch Library, *continued*

Stem Stitch. Stem stitch is useful for creating a line with no end points in it, like a flower stem. Start with a straight stitch, but don't pull the thread all the way through the fabric. Instead, gently hold the thread to the side, creating an arch. Bring your needle up between the ends of the arch. Now pull the thread all the way through the fabric, pulling the arch flat. Make another straight stitch, holding the thread to the side to make a small arch. Bring your needle up between the ends of the arch, using the same hole as the end of the arch from the first stitch. Repeat.

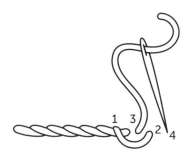

Straight Stitch (Running Stitch). This is a simple single stitch. Bring your needle through the fabric from back to front where you want the stitch to start. Then, bring your needle through the fabric from front to back where you want the stitch to end. These stitches can be placed in any direction, in groups, or used alone.

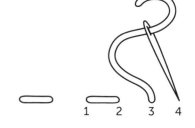

Whipped Backstitch. This is an outline stitch that makes a nice continuous line. First, stitch a row of backstitch. Then, using the same color of floss (or a different one to create a baker's twine effect), weave through the backstitches. To do this, bring your needle up through the fabric at the beginning of your row of backstitch. Guide the needle under the first stitch from right to left without entering the fabric. Repeat with the second stitch. Continue wrapping the floss around the backstitches, pulling it gently and uniformly. If the backstitches turn a corner or change direction, stitch down through the fabric to secure the floss. Then begin the wrapping process with the next section.

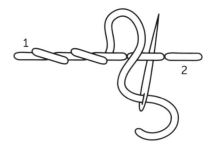

Floss Color Index

If you'd like to use the same colors that I did for these projects, here are the DMC floss color numbers so you can look for them in your local craft store. While this guide is here for your reference, you should always feel free to substitute colors or develop your own color scheme for each project!

Say It Loud
White: BLANC

On the Sunny Side
Mustard: 3820

You Got This
Red: 817
Orange: 721
Yellow: 18
Bright Green: 470
Teal: 3810
Pink: 3609
White: BLANC

Shine Bright
Mustard: 3820
Baby Pink: 963
Burnt Orange: 922
Light Green: 471
Lavender: 554
Pale Aqua: 504
Carnation Pink: 3733

Wildflower Trio
White: BLANC

Sunny Days Ahead
Black: 310
Dark Brown: 898
Bright Green: 470
Coral: 351
Salmon: 352
Yellow Green: 3348
Yellow: 18
Orange: 721

Mini Greenhouse
Black: 310
Mustard: 3820
Light Jade: 320
Forest Green: 987
Yellow Green: 3348
Bright Green: 470

Fresh as a Daisy
White: BLANC
Peach: 754
White Tapestry Wool: BLANC

Meet Me at the Farmers' Market
Tan: 436
Jade Green: 367
Coral: 351
Burnt Orange: 922
Ivory: ECRU
Yellow: 18
Dark Brown: 898
Mustard: 3820
Yellow Green: 3348
Blue: 793
Salmon: 352

Summer Citrus
White: BLANC
Bright Green: 470
Forest Green: 987
Burnt Orange: 922
Salmon: 352
Yellow: 18

Cozy Chickens
Black: 310
Ivory: ECRU
Baby Pink: 963
Burnt Orange: 922
Carnation Pink: 3733

Good Things Take Time
Tan: 436
Bright Green: 470
Salmon: 352
Ivory: ECRU
White: BLANC
Lavender: 554
Baby Pink: 963
Burnt Orange: 922
Pink: 3609
Yellow: 18
Light Jade: 320

Leaf Guide
White: BLANC

Woodland Wonders
Coral: 351
Ivory: ECRU
Yellow Green: 3348
Yellow: 18
Olive Green: 469
Jade Green: 367

Brilliant Butterfly
Metallic Gold: G3821
Mustard: 3820
Burnt Orange: 922
Yellow Green: 3348
Bright Green: 470
Black: 310
Ivory: ECRU
Salmon: 352
Coral: 351

My Happy Place
Gray: 646
Light Apricot: 3770
Blue: 793
Dark Brown: 898
Forest Green: 987
Mustard: 3820

Color Theory

There is both an art and a science behind choosing your floss and fabric colors to customize a design. The art of the process is simply noticing which colors draw you in and "look nice" together. You can also apply science to color selection with some basic color theory. Have fun choosing colors for the projects, or use the Floss Color Index on page 150 to see the specific floss color numbers I chose.

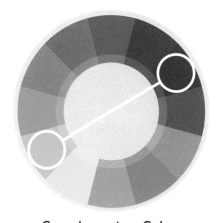

Complementary Colors
Two colors directly opposite each other
on the color wheel

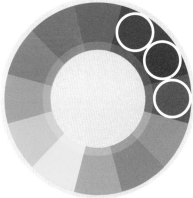

Analogous Colors
Three colors next to each other
on the color wheel

Triadic Colors
Three colors equally spaced from
one other on the color wheel

Monochromatic Colors
A collection of tints, shades, and tones of one color

Patterns

In the coming pages, you will find patterns for all of the projects in this book. I hope they will bring you many hours of happy stitching! Please see page 20 for tips on how to transfer the patterns.

Say It Loud pattern, instructions on page 38

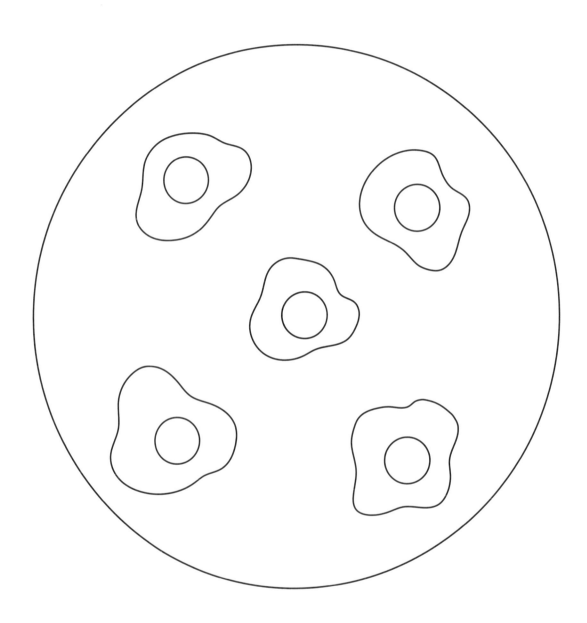

On the Sunny Side pattern, instructions on page 44

You Got This pattern, instructions on page 50

Shine Bright pattern, instructions on page 56

Wildflower Study pattern, instructions on page 64

Sunny Days Ahead pattern, instructions on page 70

Miniature Greenhouse pattern, instructions on page 76

Woodland Wonders pattern, instructions on page 124

Fresh as a Daisy pattern, instructions on page 84

Meet Me at the Farmers' Market pattern, instructions on page 92

Summer Citrus pattern, instructions on page 98

Cozy Chickens pattern, instructions on page 104

Sweater pattern
for appliqué

Good Things Take Time pattern, instructions on page 110

Leaf Guide pattern, instructions on page 118

Brilliant Butterfly pattern, instructions on page 130

My Happy Place pattern, instructions on page 136

Index

BETTER DAY BOOKS®

HAPPY • CREATIVE • CURATED

Business is personal at Better Day Books. We were founded on the belief that all people are creative and that making things by hand is inherently good for us. It's important to us that you know how much we appreciate your support. The book you are holding in your hands was crafted with the artistic passion of the author and brought to life by a team of wildly enthusiastic creatives who believed it could inspire you. If it did, please drop us a line and let us know about it. Connect with us on Instagram, post a photo of your art, and let us know what other creative pursuits you are interested in learning about. It all matters to us. You're kind of a big deal.

it's a good day to have a better day!®

www.betterdaybooks.com
better_day_books